W9-ATH-572

ROOSTER!

A Tribute to Pheasant Hunting in North America

NORTH★AMERICAN★HUNTING★CLUB

Datus Proper about to shoot a Big Sky rooster.

Copyright © 2003 by Dale C. Spartas
Text copyright © 2003 by the authors
Published by DCS Publishing, Bozeman, Montana
All rights reserved. No part of this book may be reproduced, stored, or transmitted in any form or by any means without the prior permission of the publisher, except for brief excerpts for reviews.
ROOSTER! A Tribute to Pheasant Hunting in North America
Printed in South Korea

For autographed and inscribed copies of ROOSTER!
Write to Dale C. Spartas at DCS Photo, Inc., PO Box 1367, Bozeman, MT 59771,
or call 406-585-2244, fax 406-585-0038, or visit www.spartasphoto.com.

For custom prints of the photographs:
Individual custom prints of the photographs in *ROOSTER!* and Dale's images are available directly from the photographer. Dale is also available for photo shoots of your lodge, hunt, dogs, horses, and family and friends. Write to Dale C. Spartas at DCS Photo, Inc., PO Box 1367, Bozeman, MT 59771, or call 406-585-2244, fax 406-585-0038, or visit www.spartasphoto.com.

10 9 8 7 6 5 4
ISBN 1-931832-53-6
North American Hunting Club, 12301 Whitewater Drive, Minnetonka, MN 55343

Contents

Dedication

Last fall with the help of the Pheasants Forever's national staff, field biologists, and volunteers, I embarked on a wonderful three-week sojourn to *Pheasants Forever Land*. The title is a play on Peter Pan's Never-Never Land. Ironically 20 years ago most people thought that the pheasants would never return. These strong beliefs and convictions led to Pheasants Forever (PF) being referred to as *"Pheasants Maybe."*

Thanks to a handful of forward thinking individuals who stopped talking about the problem and became a "BIG" part of the solution, the *Longtailed Birds* have returned in abundance to the heartland. Other than the wonderful realization of the birds' return and a few memorable days afield due to the PF movement—*and it is a movement*—the most significant aspect of the trip was the people. The PF volunteer members, guides, outfitters, tourism personal, farmers, and ranchers I encountered opened my eyes and reinstilled my faith in Americans and the American Way, which, fortunately, still has a solid foundation and strong hold in the Heartland of this great country.

ROOSTER *is dedicated to the founders of Pheasants Forever,*
its chapters and volunteers who give their talent, time, and
energy to conservation efforts and projects,
and to all the forward thinking hunter conservationists
who have worked and succeeded in preserving and
enhancing the natural resources of their countries.

DALE C. SPARTAS
BOZEMAN, MONTANA

Trip to Pheasants Forever Land

Dale C. Spartas

ON OCTOBER 12, 2003, I EMBARKED ON A THREE-WEEK, 3,100-mile trip to *Pheasants Forever Land*. I photographed and hunted across South Dakota, through a large portion of Iowa and southwestern Minnesota, and back across South Dakota. The trip was an enlightening insight into the dedication and the effectiveness of the Pheasants Forever (PF) movement and the heartland of America. Being on assignment for *Pheasants Forever* magazine and working on this book, I attended several PF banquets, and I met, stayed with, and hunted with Pheasants Forever volunteers, biologists, several guides, the Veurinks of Veurink's Dakota Outdoors, and some old friends Michael McIntosh, Dan Foster, and Dr. Charlie Harvey.

The accommodations covered the gamut from elegant to the back of my Suburban. In Harrold, South Dakota, the Tumbleweed Lodge is stately, well-appointed, serves excellent cuisine, and has a beautiful, well-stocked bar with a nice wine selection. "Hunters Welcome" signs graced the entrances of the Kelly Inn in Mitchell, South Dakota, and the Ramkota Hotel in Aberdeen, South Dakota. Both had lists of hunting properties and guide services and bowls of dog bones at the check-in counter. My Brittany liked the Ramkota's while my pointer preferred the Kelly's bones, and my Labrador liked them both.

I attended "Hunter's Breakfast" at The United Church of Christ in Mitchell and at the fire hall in Sigourney, Iowa. After a hardy breakfast at the church, Randy Erickson and his 12-year-old son Joshua took me and my friend Jarod Highberg to their truck and showed us a bolt action .410 shotgun that Josh had shot his first rooster with the week before at a youth hunt. Interestingly, Joshua's father and grandfather had shot their first roosters with the same gun. The photograph of Randy

(LEFT) A family's proud moment: 12-year-old A.J. looks up at his dad, Jeff VanDerBeek, who is holding A.J.'s second rooster of his life.

(RIGHT) Three-generation gun: Randy and Joshua Erickson admire a bolt-action .410 with which both of them and Joshua's grandfather harvested their first pheasants.

Randy Erickson serves breakfast to pheasant hunters at the United Church of Christ in Mitchell. Pheasant hunters are appreciated and welcomed in South Dakota, where they infuse the economy with $150 million annually.

The commencement of the Shawd Family Hunt near Mitchell, South Dakota. Every year members of the Shawd family gather at the family farm to hunt the opening weekend of the pheasant season. The morning hunt is followed by a potluck buffet, which takes precedence over the hunt. Hunting, although important, is a just a small part of this annual family reunion.

and Joshua admiring the .410 is lit with pride and highlighted in the love and bond of family tradition. Fittingly, the sun peaked through the clouds when I was taking the photograph.

Pam Van Dover and the staff of the Mitchell Convention & Visitor Bureau (CVB) pulled out all the stops. Through Pam's efforts I was afforded the pleasurable opportunity of attending the Shawd Family Hunt and hunting at Veurink's Dakota Outdoors with the Veurink family on their pheasant-laden farm.

Iowa was better than I imagined it could be. While much of Iowa is flat and planted in corn, there are rolling hills, wood lots, and creek bottoms. Vast fields of knee-high switch grass undulated in the wind. Lowlands and waterways of waist- and even head-high big and little bluestem and Indian grass made for tough going and abundant birds. Don Borts, a former Soil Conservation Service conservationist, manages his farm for pheasants. The majority of Don's farm is planted in CRP interlaced with food plots of corn and sorghum mixed with switch and gamut prairie grass to provide ground cover for the birds, cottontails, and deer.

A significant part of Don and Dorthea Borts' harvest is allowing family, friends, and neighbors to hunt and enjoy their farm.

While Don and his aging black and white mongrel Cindy were along for the entire day's hunt, I am not sure if he ever loaded his beautiful Browning Upland Special over/under. He'd tell us where to hunt, how to hunt an area, and then stand back and take it all in, enjoying himself as much if not more than the hunter. He never had to correct or yell at his dog, he never got ahead or behind the hunters, and he never missed! His contented glow and smile actualized that *"It is in giving that we receive."* Don took me to the center of one of his fields where he had mowed 10-foot-wide paths to the south, north, east, and west. He told me that he often goes out to the center of the cross and watches the pheasants, rabbits, and deer come out to the paths at the end of the day.

I spent a morning hunting with Jeff and Janet VanDerBeek and their two boys, A.J. and Brook, and their Brittanys and English setter near Oskaloosa, Iowa. Jeff is president of the Mahaska County PF Chapter and the whole family is involved and dedicated to the cause. It was A.J.'s second hunt. I saw him down one rooster his dad had missed and centered another that flushed from a thick creek bottom at the end of a drive, presenting a high crossing left-to-right shot. During the hunt A.J. mishandled his gun and in this case it was one strike and you are out! Jeff had him unload his gun for the rest of the hunt.

After hunting we cleaned a couple of birds and grilled them in the field for lunch and played with Scott's new 10-week-old Labrador pup. The only downside to the experience was that two roosters were hit but never recovered. We searched both areas with the aid of four dogs for more than 20 minutes and returned to the site at the end of the hunt for another look to no avail.

If you build it they will come

Bad weather had moved in and there were a couple of inches of heavy snow when I pulled into Ken Snyder's beautiful log home in Carroll County, Iowa. Ken is very involved with PF, an ardent conservationist, and a mover and shaker within the local, county, and state government. He raises, harvests, and sells prairie grass seed and beautiful hunting Weimaraners. Early the next morning we met Ken's partner in conservation, Larry Greving, and hunted Larry's farm. There were two inches of heavy wet snow and it was foggy, real foggy. That morning we hunted behind a beautiful "blue" Weimaraner, Misty, and Bell, a brush-busting Wirehair.

Larry's farm is a model of habitat management. It has shelterbelts, food plots, creek bottoms, and ditches with 40-foot buffer zones of big blue stem and willows—and lots of pheasants. We lunched at a small diner where the only patrons were pheasant hunters; lunch was nine bucks for the three of us. After lunch we hunted Larry's Springers which did a great job of flushing and

Farmer/outfitter Cal Veurink attends to a few last minute chores before the hunt.

Pipes, a yellow Lab, delivers a beautiful rooster to Rob Veurink at Veurink's Dakota Outdoors near Corsica, South Dakota.

retrieving pheasants. We moved more than 100 pheasants and two very nice whitetail bucks on 285 acres in four hours of hunting.

Happy hunters: Shawd family hunters and their springer spaniels with roosters taken during their afternoon hunt.

From Carroll County I drove north to Okoboji and the Iowa Great Lakes where I hooked up with Jerry Robinson and Dick Lineweaver. Both are Life Members of Pheasants Forever, with Dick being one of PF's first Lifers. The Spirit Lake and Okoboji region of Iowa is remarkable in that there is more than 20,000 acres of public land that is managed and available for recreational use and hunting. The Iowa DNR, Ducks Unlimited, Pheasants Forever, and the Iowa Natural Heritage Foundation have purchased and continue to purchase land and manage it for wildlife and recreation. The three areas we hunted provided excellent opportunities for waterfowl, deer, and pheasant hunting.

The network of public land available to hunters is vast and luckily Jerry, a retired school principal, knew it well. We hunted with his Elhew pointer Koti who did an excellent job, although we missed half the birds she found, trailed, and held for us. **The Iowa Great Lakes region is rich in hunting heritage, tradition, and "habitat" due to men like Ding Darling, Dick Lineweaver, Jerry Robinson, and countless others who stopped talking about the problem, rolled up their sleeves, reached into their back pocket, and became part of the solution.**

Southwestern Minnesota

The third morning in Okoboji the sun came out for the first time in nine days on my trip. Being a photographer my moods are affected by poor lighting and I was feeling pretty down until I stepped onto the Robinson's porch and saw and felt the sun. I ran inside and asked Jerry how soon he could be ready? He said, "I'm all ready to go and waiting on you." Twenty minutes later we were hunting a big CRP field and I took some wonderful imagery of Jerry and Koti afield on a beautiful October morning in the land of corn and ditch parrots.

After lunch and bidding Jerry and Susan goodbye, I drove north across the Iowa border to Worthington, Minnesota where, I met Les Johnson and hunted his family farm with his Labradors Rocky and Sunny. On the drive to the farm I noticed that much of the countryside was intensely farmed and relatively void of wildlife habitat. Eventually we came to a joint project of the Lake Bella Watershed District and the Nobles County PF Chapter. The project consists of a square mile (640 acres) of upland habitat surrounding a 160-acre lake. There are extensive buffer zones and shelterbelt plantings of white willow, ash, plum, and Redosher dogwood, along with thick spruce, pine, and cedar trees, and big bluestem and switch grass, providing roosting, resting, and nesting habitat for a myriad of wildlife. Next we visited the Peterson Wildlife Management Area. The 160-acre Peterson WMA is part of the same watershed system as Lake Bella and was purchased by the Nobles County Chapter of Pheasants Forever and then turned over to the Minnesota Department of Natural Resources for long-term management. While these areas are excellent models of wildlife habitat, Les told me that 85 to 90 percent of the county's wetlands had been drained.

Les Johnson's farm is a model in wildlife management containing all the necessary ingredients for upland birds, small game, deer, and many other species. The majority of the property was in long stem prairie grass with several large plum thickets, honeysuckle, willows, corn, and caricana. Within moments of stepping into the cover, "out of range" pheasants started flushing. We worked along a fence line and up a hill and through thick CRP, pushing birds into the sun. Finally a big rooster flushed and flew back toward Les, presenting an easy crossing shot. I witnessed the flush, Les swinging on the rooster, and the rooster crumple, hearing the shot a second later and then watching Rocky pick up the bird and deliver it to Les. Throughout the hunt Les was presented with numerous chances but it wasn't until my pointer Ruby nailed a tightly holding rooster that Les filled his two-cock Minnesota limit. Back at the truck I told Les that we moved 50 birds and he agreed, and he said that 10 years ago when he took over the farm he would have been lucky to see one or two pheasants.

On this trip more than ever before, the taking of birds played third fiddle to the people, places, and experience.

(FOLLOWING PAGE) *T. R. McClellan folds a cock bird over a CRP field on a windy afternoon (note the contrail of feathers) in North Dakota.*

(FAR LEFT) Yellow maple leaves near Dalton, Minnesota. Autumn colors add to the hunting experience.

(ABOVE) Bob Emery hunts with Rose, a red setter, near Bozeman, Montana.

(LEFT) T.R. McClellan admires a pair of roosters that fell to his 20-gauge Ruger Red Label.

The Thing About Pheasants

Michael McIntosh

I HAVE SHOT PHEASANTS AS DRIVEN GAME or walked them up on three continents, in five countries, and in more states of the US than I can remember. I couldn't even guess what the total body count

... a big, circus-colored rooster is about as magical as a bird can be.

might be, and once in a while the thought crosses my mind that I would not feel devastated if I never shot another.

This thought comes, of course, when I am not among a line of guns with 40-yard birds streaming overhead and when I am not pushing my way into some cornfield, coulee, or farmland slough. At those times, a big, circus-colored rooster is about as magical as a bird can be. Even a hen, which is fair game in European driven shooting and on some American preserves, can be a challenging target when she comes barreling over the line, wings pounding and the wind up her tail.

Never shoot another pheasant? Perish the thought. There's just something about pheasants.

Size is part of it. They are the largest upland game bird that is truly widespread across the world. My heart will always belong to bobwhite quail, but I cannot deny a certain fierce, atavistic satisfaction in hearing a three-pound rooster come crashing down and in how he feels in the game-pocket of my vest.

The satisfaction is even keener if I've managed to get him inside the range of my gun despite his best efforts to give me the slip—because there's no bird slipperier. You can't sneak up on a pheasant. He knows you're there the moment you step out of the truck, because his hearing is nothing short of phenomenal. During World War I, English gamekeepers documented unmistakable reactions by their penned pheasants to cannonfire on the European continent, more than 300 miles away.

A tightly holding rooster flushes from beneath Roger Keckeissen's foot in front of Rose, a Brittany who remains steady to the flush. Although presenting "easy, out-in-the-open shots," roosters that flush from underfoot often startle hunters and are frequently missed.

A young rooster might burrow into the thickest cover he can find and skulk until you simply get too close for comfort. An older one is apt to bugger off at the first hint that you're headed his way.

A couple of years ago, I was hunting in eastern South Dakota with a group large enough that we could use the classic walk-and-block approach. It's the only way to effectively hunt big cover, where one or two hunters wouldn't stand a chance. Anyway, it was my turn to be a blocker, at the end of a strip of standing corn a good half-mile long. The lay of the land was such that I could see the walkers all the way. They hadn't gone 50 feet before a rooster stuck his head out of the grass at my end, failed to notice me standing by a corner-post, and immediately quit the scene. He flushed just high enough to clear the top strand of the fence and was heading north as hard as he could go when he ran into an ounce of No. 5s that I put in his way.

Michael McGuire and Tootsie, a German Shorthair, hunt dense cover along a lake.

Star, John Millington's stylish English pointer, pins a rooster and bites her lip in anticipation of the flush at the Mashomack Club in Pine Plains, New York.

I have never seen a more beautiful bird—huge-bodied and long-tailed, gaudy as a casino, spurs long and ivory-colored at the tips. I figured him at three years old. A third-year wild rooster is a patriarch, and he doesn't get that way by sitting around waiting for somebody to boot him up. This old chap clearly knew there was danger in the field, even at half a mile away, and he wanted no part of it. His mistake was not being as observant as he might have been. I feel grateful for that, because now I can look at him every day as he stands on a bookcase in my office.

By one of those twists of coincidence that happen now and then, one of my partners killed a carbon-copy rooster in the same field this year. I'd like to believe it was one of my old boy's sons, and that his knack for survival runs rich in the gene pool thereabouts.

Just about any pheasant's penchant for survival is impressive, and all the more so when you realize they did not evolve in North America. They haven't yet figured out our native grouses' trick of burrowing into snow to escape blizzards. A lot of pheasants die out here on the plains every winter because they insist on staying on top of the snow as it accumulates, but enough survive that the population rebounds wherever the habitat allows. Cold, rainy weather during the nesting season probably kills more pheasants as chicks than succumb to any prairie

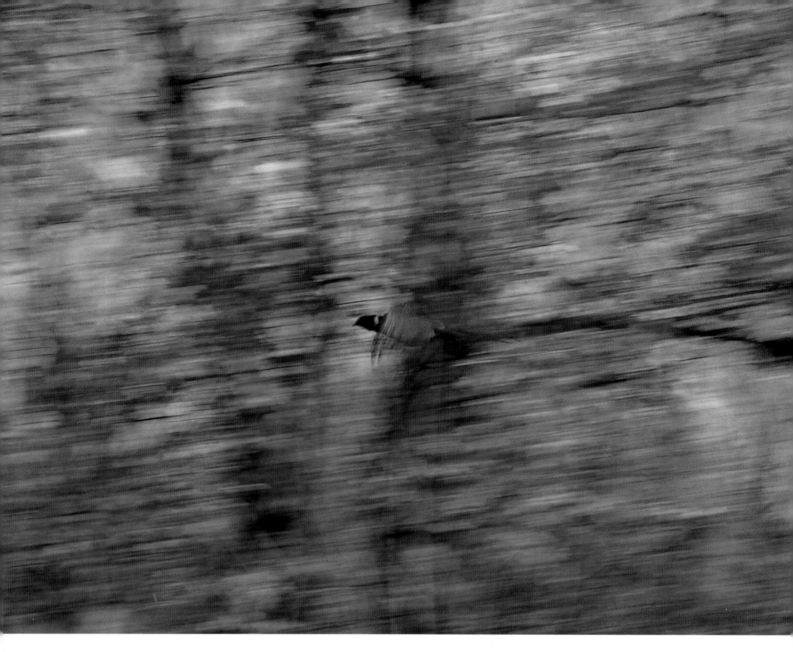

winter—and prairie winters can be brutal enough
that it's a wonder anything can make it through till
spring.

*A rooster streaks through fall foliage
in northern Iowa.*

Prairie chickens are the most obvious comparator
with pheasants, because pheasants, as amenable to agriculture as the
chicken is not, now occupy much the same range that chickens once did. This is good
zoogeography, but when I think of the pheasant's spirit and his sheer determination to survive in
this environment, I think of buffalo instead.

I've never shot a buffalo, but I have a good notion of what it would take to put down an
animal that's larger than most automobiles. Having shot a lot of pheasants, I know exactly
what's required to take one down for the count.

The first requisite is judgement, followed closely by some ability to shoot and a cartridge
that's up to the task.

Killing a pheasant can be easy or difficult, depending on how he presents himself. Flying
toward you, as in driven shooting, all his vitals are exposed—head, breast, belly, wings,
everything. A crossing shot offers most of the same advantages. Going away is a different story.
The broad, bony plate of a pheasant's back is virtual armor. In a lot of going-away shots, his

Willy, Dale Sweetser's classy Chesapeake Bay retriever, proudly holds a magnificent rooster pheasant.

body shields his head. His legs aren't very exposed, either—and unless you deliver an instantly killing shot, a pheasant with two good legs is likely to be one you don't retrieve.

Judgement means picking your shots. I'm not hesitant about shooting at even 50-yard birds if they're coming toward me, because I know that a good pattern of relatively small shot is sufficient. My comfort range with crossers is shorter, perhaps 35 yards at most. If I can see the bird's head, I'm confident that I can deliver a killing blow at that distance. But a pheasant flying straight away has to be within about 25 yards or I don't take the shot. It's not that I can't hit him; it's that I can't be as certain of bringing him down and finding him where he falls.

Pheasants tempt sloppy shooting, by which I mean focusing on the whole bird or being distracted by that long, streaming tail instead of concentrating on the part that will repay a well-placed shot. This, of course, means the front half. Stretch an average rooster out straight—place him, in other words, in the posture he assumes when he's flying—and he'll measure close to three feet from beak to tail-tip. How could you possibly miss something that size? There's a good chance you won't miss, but if you put the center of your pattern on the rearward two feet, there's an equally good chance he'll fly off carrying enough pellets to die, but not soon and not where you'll be able to recover him.

Fortunately, a cock pheasant has two good places for centering your visual focus—a white neck-ring and a bright-red patch on either side of his head. Concentrate on those, forget about the rest of the bird, and if you can place the shot where your eyes are looking, you'll pick up a pheasant that is satisfyingly dead.

Hunters drive a big, brushy creek bottom on the North Dakota-Montana border. The benches above the creek are planted in wheat, and this creek bottom yielded Hungarian partridge, sharptail grouse, and pheasants.

Just as there is a significant contrast between the birds of opening day and late season, there is a substantial difference between wild pheasants and those reared for release on shooting preserves. And to take it a step further, there's a difference between either of those and the birds reared in England and Europe for driven shooting. For the most part, they're all the same bird genetically, but they offer a remarkably wide set of contrasts when it comes to shooting.

The typical game-farm pheasant is an accommodating creature, generally willing to stick tight in the presence of both a pointing dog and a hunter. Under those circumstances, an appropriate pheasant gun can be just about anything that goes *bang*. I couldn't begin to count how many I've shot with a 28-gauge and three-quarters-ounce of No. 7½, or even No. 8s. Hit them well and they tend to come down dead.

I've done the same with wild birds during the first day or two of a season, but only by carefully picking the shots I'm willing to take. Opening-day roosters can be sophomorically credulous, not much warier than birds reared under wire—but they're still wild birds. They may be dopey, but they're physically tough to a level that game-farm birds usually aren't. That means the 28-gauge stays in the safe, because I want an ounce of heavier shot, No. 6s at least, maybe even No. 5s. My opening-weekend pheasant gun might be my favorite 20 or my lightest 12. I don't happen to own a 16-gauge at the moment, but if I did, I'd be the cat's pajamas early on.

A 16 can be good later as well, but in my mind pheasant hunting becomes a 12-gauge game after the season's been open for a couple of weeks. It doesn't take much hunting pressure to turn a rooster from Clem Cadiddlehopper to James Bond. All he has to do is survive.

Not being a turkey hunter, I can't comment on *Meleagris's* legendary reputation for being sly and hardy—but **I can't believe there's anything in the uplands wilier nor more tenacious of life than a cock pheasant.** Fringe a grouse with a few pellets of small shot and he's likely to die. Even if he doesn't, the chances are way better than even that you or your dog will find him right where he fell.

Not so a pheasant. The first problem will be getting close enough to have a reasonable shot, and if you do, you'll have to give him something more than a love-pat. Late-season pheasants demand a gun and a load capable of both reach and punch. Especially punch. You can hit him hard, but if you don't break a wing the last thing you're apt to see is his rear-end disappearing over the next hill. Or you can break a wing, but if you don't break at least one leg as well he can hit the ground like a bowling ball and in the next instant take off on foot in a sprint that some dogs are hard-pressed to match. **He'll burrow into the**

Brian Fay hunts a cottonwood bottom with Labrador retrievers Will and Chip.

grass, slither down a badger hole, swim a creek, do whatever he can possibly do to get away—and if that doesn't work, he'll be just as happy to use the last ounce of his energy to kick the hell out of you or your dog. I don't know if you've ever been spurred by a pheasant, but I have, and I'm here to tell you he can draw some blood. My good friend Dale Spartas refers to pheasants as the "ultimate survivalists."

Given the bird's swashbuckling attitude and personality of a back-alley thug, it's not hard to understand why some pheasant hunters go armed for bear. I have a habit of picking up fired cases I run across while hunting, partly because I don't like litter and partly out of curiosity to see what my colleagues are shooting. Last fall I found everything from a target load of No. 8s to a three-inch 12-gauge hull that once contained nearly two ounces of No. 2s.

Somewhere between too little and too much lies a practical medium, and though I am an ardent champion of light loads for just about everything, wild pheasants in the late season are not among them. For one thing, they're just too tough, too muscular, too willfully determined to cling to the faintest spark of life.

Pheasants and I go back a long time together, about forty-five years, if memory serves. They were the second species of game bird I ever hunted, second partly because my Dad loved bobwhite quail almost to distraction and partly because there were virtually no pheasants in the part of Iowa where we lived when I was a kid. Nowadays, it might seem hard to imagine that in the 1950s there wasn't even an open pheasant season in the two southernmost tiers of counties in Iowa, but it's true.

Pheasants were trophy birds to us, available only by taking a "hunting trip," which meant driving a hundred miles or so and being gone overnight. That was big-time stuff, and we only did it once or twice a season. Quail were the staple. Pheasants were spectacle, production, adventure, all of an Aristotelian scope.

And in some ways, they still are. Pheasants do not touch my soul as quail do, and in a typical year I'll usually spend more time fooling with grouse of one sort or another, but pheasants forever tease my mind.

Last season I spent more time hunting pheasants than usual—from the bumpkins of opening weekend to the brigands of winter, and I shot some driven birds in Europe as well. In all, it served to remind me that they are the most demanding of upland birds—in terms of effort, tactics, equipment, skill, and at times even the dose of sheer luck required just to get an opportunity to make a hit or a miss. I remembered once again how my old friend John Madson described late-season pheasants as "hunting with all the fat rendered away, and reduced to the clean white bone." It's true, and those cold, hard, bony days can be immensely satisfying or cruelly frustrating, or both by turns. But either way, mess around with pheasants and you'll know you've been somewhere.

As I said, I've shot enough pheasants that the thought of shooting another sometimes fails to send a tingle up my back. But I've been at it long enough to have discovered a sovereign cure for any such thought. It's called pheasant season.

A young-of-the-year rooster flies across a sagebrush flat in Montana.

The Pheasant Life

Jim Wooley

Pheasants Forever Senior Wildlife Biologist

FOR CENTURIES, PHEASANTS HAVE HELD A SPECIAL MYSTIQUE. They make up an immensely important branch of the single most economically significant family of birds, the Galliformes. This group includes

> *Pheasants likely rank as the most introduced bird on the planet.*

turkeys, partridges, quail, and grouse, as well as the nearly 50 separate species of pheasants, among which is the red junglefowl—the progenitor of all domestic chickens. Pheasants likely rank as the most introduced bird on the planet and have found a home nearly everywhere they have been taken.

Pheasants of western Asian origin (black-necked subspecies from the Caucasus region between the Black and Caspian Seas) were first brought to Greece around 1300 BC, and were thereafter spread throughout Western Europe during the expansion of the Roman Empire, reaching England before the 10th Century AD. This black-necked ancestry still forms the base of most European populations, but later introductions of ring-necked pheasant varieties from Eastern China in the late 1700s also left their mark on the genetics of European populations. It was from these two distinct areas—Europe and China—and with much interbreeding of parent populations that pheasants made their way eventually to the United States.

The first North American pheasant introductions occurred in 1733 in New York. Later attempts at stocking were made

(LEFT) *A rooster pheasant with swollen waddles during the spring breeding season.*

(RIGHT) *A rooster in mating plumage clucks defiantly and beats his wings, staking claim to his territory, challenging rival males, and delighting the ladies.*

Sarah, Sue and Christo Spartas release pheasants in a field along the Yellowstone River in Montana.

in New Hampshire, New Jersey, and even at Mount Vernon by George Washington, during the first term of his presidency. These birds were black-necked varieties from stock that originated in England, and the initial efforts to introduce them were unsuccessful until the late 1800s when pheasants finally became somewhat established from New Jersey up through lower New England and Maine.

Pheasant introductions were not wildly successful in North America until 1881 when Judge Owen Denny sent 40 to 70 Chinese ring-necked pheasants back home to the Willamette Valley of Oregon from his posting as Consul General in Shanghai. The small farms and diversified cropping of the day proved almost perfect for the release and later reproduction. Just a decade later, the first US pheasant hunting season took place in Oregon with a harvest that approached a half million birds. With this spectacular success, there was an immediate rush by sportsmen to introduce pheasants throughout the nation. Birds from the successful Oregon release and from pheasant populations and private game farms in other parts of the country became the source for a multitude of stockings. By 1907, there were wild pheasant populations of varying sizes in all but nine states. Efforts to bolster populations and to fill vacant habitat continued into the 1970s, both with trap-and-transplant of wild birds and with game farm stocking in various parts of the range. The last attempt to import pheasants to fill a specific habitat niche was the effort of the Michigan Department of Natural Resources to introduce Sichuan pheasants, a subspecies of brushy and wooded habitats in China, to the Lower Peninsula of Michigan in the late 1980s and early 1990s.

Since pheasants readily interbreed, and because genetics were not a consideration in these releases, the ancestry of our North

Young cock pheasants come out of heavy cover to feed early in the evening.

American ringneck is a bit murky. It's easy to see why pheasants across the US today bear the stamp of many subspecies—the result of many attempts to expand populations and range over the past 100 years. Our ringneck is a scrappy mongrel that has traces of the English blackneck, Japanese, Mongolian, Formosan, Manchurian, Korean, and Chinese ring-necked pheasants, among other subspecies.

The range map of today's North American pheasant varies remarkably little from that of 60 years ago, although populations have declined dramatically since the bird's heyday in the middle 1900s. Today, as then, pheasants are most common in the northern half of the US, where they are found in varying numbers in most of the states between both coasts. Their range extends, at relatively low population levels, north into the prairie provinces of Canada and southward to Texas. Ringnecks have largely disappeared from New England but are found in relatively low numbers in several of the northeastern states. Small localized or regional pheasant populations occur in much of the western and southwestern US, where birds are mainly confined to wetland and riparian habitats and irrigated farmland. The Upper Midwest and the Northern Plains states— areas where the Conservation Reserve and other beneficial federal farm programs have taken hold—comprise the stronghold of the ring-necked pheasant today, with Iowa, Kansas, Minnesota, Nebraska, both Dakota's, and Montana at the head of the pack.

Population Dynamics

Old Mr. Curlyspurs is a bird with a healthy libido. After a winter of restricted movements and concentration in heavier cover, pheasants disperse to spring breeding areas that are generally less than a mile distant. Like other galliformes, pheasants are polygamous. Stimulated by increasing daylight length, roosters begin claiming breeding territories by early spring, advertising their presence by crowing and display—attempting to attract as many hens as possible. These harems of breeding hens average 3 to 4 birds, or about the normal post-hunting season sex ratio in the population. Once a mating takes place, hens are able to lay fertile eggs for about three weeks but may return to the harem to breed again daily. This is no strain for our Lothario of the meadow—during studies of pheasants in captivity, roosters have mated with nearly 50 hens without loss of fertility.

A mature hen pheasant flies across the blue Kansas sky.

Hens begin nest establishment by scratching out a nest bowl in the soil and lining it with leaves and grasses. The nesting site needs to afford good ground level concealment and overhead cover to protect the hen from predation. The first nests of the season will be found in dead erect vegetation from the previous year or in areas with an early green-up like alfalfa fields. A first clutch usually numbers 12 to 15 eggs, each egg laid about every other day, until the hen begins incubating for about 23 days until hatching, which peaks during June in much of the range. Later, the new growth in hayfields or pastures becomes important for nesting hens and for newly hatched broods.

If a nest is destroyed in the process of laying or incubation, a surviving hen may re-nest several times while attempting to produce a brood. Hens that re-nest draw heavily on body fat and protein reserves, and clutch size declines steadily with each nesting attempt, as does the condition of the

A clutch of eight-week-old pheasants feeds along a fence line in Nebraska. In much of their range, secure grassland habitat that remains undisturbed during the nesting and brood-rearing periods is the single most important limiting factor for pheasants.

A ringneck pheasant nine to ten weeks old. Young chicks face many dangers, and only about half a brood of young pheasants will survive until fall, contributing three hens and three cocks to the fall population.

hen. Unlike quail and morning doves, hen pheasants will only nest successfully once during a breeding season, bringing off a single brood. Young pheasant chicks hatch within hours of each other, dry off quickly, and are quickly led away into the surrounding cover by the hen—beginning a brood-rearing period that lasts another 12 to 14 weeks.

Annual mortality for pheasants is similar for both males and females but occurs during different times of the year. The male segment of the population is subject to heavy hunter harvest and may incur losses up to 80 percent—although a more normal mortality is 60-70 percent through the hunting season. Annual rates of loss for hens average 60-80 percent in normal years, but mortality is more evenly distributed through the seasons. Pheasants, like other wildlife, are subject to catastrophic losses—mainly from severe blizzards that may kill 90 percent of populations over large regions. The breeding biology of the pheasant, and it's prolific nature, allow it to bounce back quickly from these setbacks given favorable weather and habitat conditions.

Habitat through the Annual Cycle

Pheasants are very evident on the landscape during several seasons of the year—perhaps most often in spring when roosters display and are often seen with hens in grassy habitats and new cropland during the breeding period. In fact, throughout the year pheasants are birds of open cropland and grassland that use other adjacent habitats, as well. They are birds that do well in landscapes with a minimum of 15-20 percent undisturbed grassland cover, a significant amount of domestic grain acreage, and less than 15 percent of the area in forest.

Cool and warm season grasses and annual broad-leaved plants (forbs) play a role in other important habitat needs of pheasants during spring and summer. This complex of plants provides night roosting areas, feeding sites for

A cock pheasant hides among autumn-colored sumac leaves in Pennsylvania. For such a gaudy bird, he is amazingly well camouflaged.

chicks and adult birds, areas for daytime loafing, and cover in which to escape predators. In these early successional habitats (like new or renovated grasslands, abandoned feedlots, weedy cornfields, and food plots) pheasants can multiply rapidly, particularly when the areas undergo "managed disturbance" every few years.

During spring and summer, pheasant hens move their broods to areas of high insect numbers—places like lightly grazed pastures and hay, or old-field CRP habitats where movement by young chicks is unimpeded and bugs are abundant. Since pheasants are an "edge" species, broods and hens are often seen traveling along corridor plantings that connect separated habitats. Woody draws, brushy fence rows, or small shrub plantings of wild plum, choke cherry, or ninebark provide loafing cover for broods in daylight hours and a corridor to move to secure grassy cover for the evening. These areas provide excellent escape habitats, as do warm-season native grasses and standing crop.

As fall approaches, cover is rapidly removed by agricultural harvest activities and pheasants find their movements dictated by the lack of habitat. Pheasants continue to roost in idle fields during the evenings and may spend the day in standing corn or other rowcrops until the crops are removed. As temperatures fall, pheasants need heavier cover that will capture snow and cut winter winds, while protecting leeward grasses for roosting.

Cover is eliminated by farming in late fall and as conditions become much more severe during winter, the protective nature of habitat on the landscape changes. Grain stubble and weed patches that concealed feeding birds during fall are soon buried in blowing snow. Pheasants

(ABOVE) *Pheasants love thick, woody-stem cover, the thicker the better.*

(LEFT) *A pair of roosters peeks out of the grass at Tumbleweed Lodge in Harrold, South Dakota.*

29

concentrate in limited heavy roosting cover and venture only as far as needed—feeding within a half mile from cover, even if abundant food exists beyond that range. Native warm-season grasses such as big bluestem, indiangrass, and switchgrass are excellent choices for winter roosting cover

(ABOVE) Prime pheasant habitat: Three Cross Ranch near Rapelje, Montana.

(RIGHT) Although the hen pheasant does not exhibit the breathtaking brilliance of a rooster, she is beautiful in her own right.

under these conditions. These grasses have rigid stalks that stand up to snow or lodge so they are still useful for roosting cover. Food patches near these islands of habitat establish safe foraging patterns, restrict unnecessary movements, and provide dependable food to carry female birds through the winter in good condition.

Tradition: Hunting With Family & Friends

Jim Wooley

It is October, and the air is adrift with the sharp scents of fallen leaves, earth freshly turned, and apples gone by. In the field, standing corn rustles dryly, awaiting the rumble of combines that will come to pluck the ears, and with them lift the bounty of the land. Frost paints the waterways and fence rows each morning now, as the lazy warmth of early autumn gives way and turns crisp across the grain belt. And, once again, as has happened for decades, families begin to gather— honoring a custom generations in the making. In late autumn, pheasant hunting is the glue that binds loved ones far separated, bringing them back to take part in a wholesome reunion at the ebbing of the year—the tradition of chasing the ringneck together, a continuation of the harvest of the land. And in the pursuit of this vivid bird, this quarry with attitude, those who seek the pheasant find the burdens of modern life broken away and laid aside at least for a while.

How many times is this episode repeated each year across the Pheasant Belt of this nation? In rural and small town homes that stretch from the lake country of New York, down through the Buckeye State and Indiana, across lower Michigan, Wisconsin, and the farms of southern Minnesota, to the pothole country of the Dakotas and west through Montana to the

... those who seek the pheasant find the burdens of modern life broken away and laid aside at least for a while.

(LEFT) *Fourteen-year-old Nate DeChaine with a pair of roosters and a big smile.*

(RIGHT) *Nate DeChaine and his dad, John, walk to the truck after Nate's first pheasant hunt. This is one of the photographer's favorite photographs.*

Palouse of Washington, then south through Colorado into Texas, back to the bulging belly of Kansas' wheat lands and up through the cornbelt of Nebraska, Iowa and Illinois—it's a familiar slice of Americana.

(LEFT) Gentleman gunner and sportsman Ted Wilbert, 79, takes an early-season rooster from Buck, a black Lab.

(RIGHT) Father and son, Bill and Bryan Zales, enjoy a day afield together. Could they be any happier?

Somewhere in the heart of the pheasant range, a pickup truck pulls in the driveway of a big, white clapboard farmhouse late in the afternoon on the eve of **Opening Day. Doors open, and families rush together—hugs and handshakes, kisses, backs slapped. And then, grins all around, as yet another vehicle turns into the drive. Sons and daughters that left the farm for a different way of life have been drawn to their roots, back to their natal home from the warren of the cities, renewing their ties with family and the land.** With them, in their children who long to hunt this bird, comes hope for the future of the sport.

Fathers and sons and daughters unpack pickup loads of hunting gear, as mothers and grandparents tote food to the house. Dogs bound from crates and, reacquainted after a year apart, race round the yard anticipating the next day's events, then loll in the shade—great, happy, flop-tongued dog smiles on their faces. Labs, Setters, Brittanys and Springers use this respite to trade good-natured insults about the merits of their masters, while Shorthairs and Goldens swap cat stories in the sun-dappled grass.

Later, towards dusk, three generations gather at the edge of the farmstead next to picked beans, to brush up shooting skills and transform a box of clays to dust. Talk turns to the bird numbers this fall, the flock of Huns that old Nils Anderssen saw by the feed mill, the prairie drought and its impact on ducks, the changes that have come to the land thereabouts. There's more CRP now, but mostly buffers, the good old fence rows are all torn out, been a lot of brush dozing that's hurt wintering habitat, but there's some bright spots too, like the new 12-row shelterbelt expansion on the home place that the Pheasants Forever chapter helped with.

A Grandfather gently reminds his youngest grandchild about the wag of a barrel, then has everyone check breeches and safeties, and delivers "the talk" for the umpteenth time to faces that

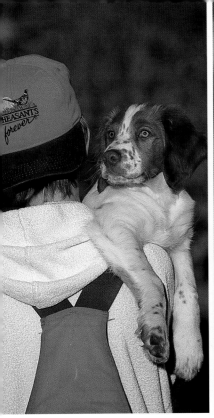

fill with brief, knowing smiles … field of fire, shooting zones, birds in the sun, staying abreast in line across the field, watching the dogs, what birds we shoot and what we don't and why, where we hunt and why we ask permission, of crossing fences safely, and watch those bulls of Haegermann's, and oh, stay out of the slough at Zilstra's 'cause it's been sold.

(LEFT) Young hopefuls, Elizabeth Spartas and Champ, a 14-week-old Brittany pup. Our youth are the future of hunting and conservation. Whenever possible, introduce children to hunting and the outdoors.

(RIGHT) Grandpa Paul Giesenhagen, Sr., teaches his grandson Paul Giesenhagen, III, how to properly mount a gun.

There's conversation about clothes and boots, snacks to bring, chokes and loads, pellet size and patterning, leading a bird crossing full tilt in a tailwind, giving the close ones a little distance before firing, and always sighting through the bird to see what lies beyond. And just as important—there's sportsmanship. It's knowing when to fire and when to defer to a hunting partner, letting the birds of questionable identity go, always giving the second effort to find downed birds, how watching the flight of "missed birds" sometimes ends in retrieving game, why fences don't get crossed without permission and emphasizing once again that in these fields there will be no competition. No one disagrees.

They know from many years past that harvesting birds *is* part of the hunt, and that is only as it should be. For this family, though, the hunt is much more. It's about the spirit of hunters at a community firehall breakfast in the dim light of early opening morning. **It's the quiet anticipation in the truck on the way to the field, deep in the dusky smell of hunting vests and dog fur. It's the prairie slough grass rippling in the breeze, the crunch of the frosted weeds beneath your boots, watching good dogs coursing heavy cover, the joshing after a shot misplaced, a stick of Grandpa's Beeman's gum, and the taste of an apple at midmorning.**

Being there is about how well Grandpa still shoots and how poorly Dad will (and oh, the fun to be had later with that!). It's the hustling excitement of a cafe full of hunters and their stories at noon. It's getting together with cousins and uncles and a friend or two, pan-fried pheasants that first night, Aunt Norah's peach cobbler and a bed that just feels so good. This pheasant opener will be different and yet the same, like all the others that came before—rich in memories that ripen with time, to be opened and sipped slowly, far down the road from these days.

And now there's time for family competition, a friendly match before the hunt. Out come the clays and the Trius Trap. White Rocks fly, and shooting tips are offered—often in jest, always unsolicited and free of charge. And amid the oddly agreeable mix of spent gunpowder and soft perfume, daughters with side-by-sides once again show brothers with pump guns what breaking birds and busting boy's chops are all about.

These youngsters have been fortunate. Someone cared enough to take them afield long before they could shoot, little feet walking with family and watching the hunt. Now they live and breathe the outdoors. They're part of a local Pheasants Forever chapter's Ringnecks program, and have been to the mentor hunt and fishing clinic the chapter sponsored. They've taken shooting safety classes in local 4-H programs, participated in an Ikes fall youth shoot, and been to a local Greenwings day to learn about waterfowl. They finagle ways to hunt, and fish, however they can.

(LEFT) *Beth Murphy with a rooster pheasant. We are beginning to see more and more women afield.*

(BELOW) *Scott Wuebber teaches proper and safe gun handling to his sons, Brian and Chris.*

(RIGHT) *With its metallic green and blue head, vibrant red waddles, snow-white ring band, and multicolored iridescent body, a rooster pheasant is stunning and beautiful.*

Careful attention guided these young minds into this tradition. That's an exception rather than the rule these days, and therein lies the problem—for youth in general and hunting in particular. **Unfortunately, the number of youngsters entering hunting traces a declining trend line.** Other competing pursuits—work, school, sports, the couch—have monopolized their time, and ours, and relegated a jaunt with a shotgun and bird dog to a backseat post. Families reduced to single parent units, without an active sportsperson, find there is no time for the outdoors and no one to teach the skills.

Much is made of family values these days. Well, values abound in the tradition of families and friends gathering to hunt pheasants on the North Dakota prairies or a Southern Iowa farm. Hunting strengthens the bridge between young and old, and feeds the interests of youth. Lessons in sportsmanship pass from older to younger generations, or from a mentor to a youngster with no teacher of his own. In hunting we promote conservation of wildlife and reverence for the land, teamwork and respect. The art of reading the land passes on. Just simple things, really, but measure the impact on a young person's life.

Those of us who hunt, whether birds, deer or ducks, sometimes forget the unspoken obligation we took up along with that shotgun so many years ago … to keep the tradition strong. Delivering on that commitment isn't difficult—it's taking your own kids hunting and bringing youngsters with less opportunity along. It means extra effort from professional folks who care for wildlife and the

(FAR LEFT) *Christo D. Spartas steadies Roscoe, a 12-week-old tricolor English setter, as the pup points a wing.*

(ABOVE) *Ross and Bill Oyler swing on a rooster that held for a point and flushed from a lightly grazed pasture.*

(RIGHT) *Avid bird hunters Brian and Greg Fay with a rooster and Rita, Greg's Boykin spaniel. Boykins have been a rare sight in pheasant country but are rapidly gaining in popularity.*

(LEFT) *Old pros Larry Michnevich and Purdey, a 13-year-old Brittany.*

(ABOVE) *The VanDerBeek family with their dogs during Iowa's 2002 pheasant opener. Jeff is the president of the Mahaska County Chapter of Pheasants Forever in Oskaloosa, Iowa, and the entire family is involved PF projects.*

(RIGHT) *Recalling a great hunt, Warren Schlichting, Scott Wyckoff, Bob Emery, and George Davis yuck it up after a successful pheasant hunt in North Dakota.*

land, more teamwork among conservation groups, a willingness to reach out to youth to communicate the passion of hunting and being afield.

Simple things—an experienced hand coaching a young shooter in the safety and ethics of the hunt, gifting a young person with a knowledge of habitat and wild things, gently encouraging a youngster with his first pup, opening doors closed to recreational access, being someone to go hunting with. How important can these simple things be? Ask a 14 year old—the new dog's mug full of pheasant feathers, a father's hand on his shoulder, first bird in the game pouch warm against his back, a friend at his side who has never hunted before—with his first ring-neck, as well. Have you passed on what was given you? Have you made a difference? Are they on the right path? Look at the light dancing in their eyes. Read your answer in the grins on their faces.

Pheasant Dogs

Dave Carty

W E'D BEEN COMBING THE BANKS OF THE CANAL for half an hour when Poke put his nose to smoking pheasant scent and beelined upstream.

Want a geat pheasant dog? Then hunt him a lot.

But the bird had different ideas about being reduced to possession. I caught a glimpse of my bull-shouldered little springer as he disappeared into the brush, his stub of a tail trembling like a sinner at a revival meeting. I hitched up my vest and hobbled after him as fast as my gimpy knees would allow.

And then I got a break. For reasons I'll never understand—and for reasons the bird undoubtedly regretted—he decided to make a stand in a patch of cattails. My springer spun to a stop, stared hard at the grass at his feet, and then pounced in a long, flat arc. When he came down again, the bird rocketed up from beneath him. I scratched it down as it sailed over the canal.

What kept my spaniel hot on that pheasant's trail for 200 yards? Experience. Sure, training and instinct played an important part, but it was his experience that ultimately put that rooster in the back of my vest.

Want a great pheasant dog? Then hunt him a *lot*. Before I talk about the various breeds—and they all have their pros and cons—you have to understand that no dog will live up to his potential if you hunt him only five or six days a year. That's not to say he won't become an adequate bird finder, or that you should throw in the towel and take up bowling. But assuming your dog has the right genes, it's field experience and field experience alone that will turn him into a top-notch rooster rouster—and that's true no matter what kind of dog you ultimately settle on.

(LEFT) *Beam, a springer spaniel, proudly delivers the rooster it retrieved.*

(RIGHT) *Scott Peterson combs burrs out of the tail of Brandy, a golden retriever, at Lone Tree Wildlife Management Area in North Dakota.*

(TOP) *Not to be denied: Oscar, a springer spaniel, runs in with a rooster he retrieved from across the Gallatin River in Montana.*

(LEFT) *Springer spaniels Rusty and Libby pose with five roosters near Letcher, South Dakota.*

Luckily for me, my more or less unemployable nature allows me to hunt fifty or sixty days a year, and although I don't always hunt pheasants in my spare time, my dogs and I are always hunting

(FEFT) *Rita, a Boykin spaniel, sits next to a rooster.*

(RIGHT) *Larry Michnevich hunts a huge CRP field with his springer spaniel.*

something. But, unlike me, you don't have to carry a shotgun to "hunt" over your dog. Running him in cover year around will allow him to develop his skills at finding and trailing pheasants even if you can't shoot them. Ditto for working your dogs on penned quail or pigeons. True, penned birds rarely behave like wild birds, but *any* kind of bird work is better than nothing. And if all else fails, farm him out to a professional trainer. They're not inexpensive, but a good pro will get your dog into more birds in a week than you'll get him into in a season.

Spaniels

Springers are considered by many to be the ultimate pheasant dog. Those who feel this way won't get an argument from me. Poke was so driven to hunt that he was continually running into trees and fence posts. One day, as I stood in the bottom of a frozen creek bed, he suddenly hurtled over the embankment above me, spun completely over in mid air, and landed on his head at my feet. He got up with a punch-drunk look in his eyes, staggered around for a moment, and then got right back to the business at hand. *That's* drive.

When people think spaniels, they usually think springers, and there are probably more springers in the field than all the other breeds combined, although two of those breeds, cockers and Boykins, also have small but loyal followings. Cockers and Boykins are both on the small side, though, and their main disadvantage is that, with limited breeding stock in this country, it can be tough to find a hunting-oriented kennel. My suggestion? Before you buy any puppy, ask to see at least one of the parents hunt. Take them to a field and check for drive and birdyness. If it's there, you'll see it, and there's a good chance the offspring will have that birdyness, too. In fact, this is a good practice before buying a puppy of *any* breed.

Hunting over spaniels is interactive. They won't hold a bird like a pointer; instead, they'll flush it, and their bouncing, hyperactive gait makes them thrilling to watch (and an occasional pain in the neck in the house). But you have to do your part. That means staying with the dog when it's hot on the scent of a bird. Sure—you can whistle your pooch to stop and wait while you catch up with him, but the bird is under no such compunctions and may very well take that opportunity to leave the two of you in the dust. There are plenty of good reasons for teaching your spaniel to hup (sit) on the

Flying Falcon Buster sits with a cock pheasant. Flying Falcon goldens are some of the best field-bred golden retrievers in the country.

whistle, but once your dog starts making game, use the command only as a last resort. You'll be birds ahead if you adapt to your dog, rather than forcing him to adapt to you.

Addy, a black Labrador, jumps a fence with a rooster. Addy is small, only 49 pounds, and hunts energetically all day. She is a superb "hard flush" Labrador that was bred by Clint and Stephanie Krumm, who own and operate River Ready Kennels in Buffalo, Wyoming.

Spaniels are great little dogs for hunting in the thick, nasty, thorny, briary hells that, increasingly, pheasants seem to live in. Equally important, they'll retrieve dead birds from those same places, saving you hours of misery and gallons of blood transfusions. In fact, a springer's retrieving ability is one of the breed's more underrated assets. When Poke wasn't hunting pheasants, he did double duty as a serious duck fetcher, and a heck of a good one, at that.

Retrieving, in fact, is absolutely essential in a pheasant dog, which segues nicely into the next section...

Retrievers

Most folks associate retrievers with waterfowl hunting, and for good reason—it's the job they're bred for. But retrievers have been putting up pheasants for generations, and if their popularity among bird hunters is any indication, they must be doing something right.

Among retrievers, there are several popular breeds: Chesapeakes, goldens, the beautiful flat-coated retrievers, and a half dozen other breeds I've yet to see or hunt over. But Labradors are far and away the stars of the show. The reason? Their intelligence, tractability, and boundless enthusiasm.

Depending upon your priorities, though, they also have drawbacks. While a spaniel will typically dance through thick cover, a Lab will simply lower his head and plow a furrow through the middle of it. That's not true with every Lab, of course, but in my experience it's true for most of them. Both breeds get the job done, but the style points go to the spaniels. Finally, Labs, because of their sheer size, are typically methodical, slow hunters. But let's face it—the average bird hunter in this country is in his fifties. *We're* methodical and slow. A dog that matches our increasingly geriatric pace isn't necessarily a bad choice.

Perhaps one of the best reasons to hunt over Labs, though, is shown in the following anecdote, which took place in the grouse covers of Minnesota, not in the pheasant-thick cornfields of the Midwest.

Labrador retrievers come in three colors and many sizes and personalities. They are the most popular breed registered by the American Kennel Club and the most popular pheasant dogs in the world.

My friend Chris and I were hunting three dogs that trip: my springer, my Brittany, and Sunny, Chris' year-old yellow Lab. In fairness, I should mention that it was my springer that found most of the birds on that trip. But I was impressed—more than I thought I'd be—by Sunny's dogged persistence in rooting out game. The little guy simply wouldn't quit. At an age when many dogs are still trying to figure out how to hunt, Sunny knew all about bird scent and was bound and determined to go where his nose was leading him. Into the briars? Didn't matter. Through muddy, boot-sucking swamps? Much to our reluctance, that didn't matter, either. But most impressive was the pup's retrieving ability. I don't recall our ever losing a grouse or woodcock, although several times my Brittany simply turned up her nose at fallen birds and continued to hunt. Not Sunny. He retrieved every bird Chris shot over him and some of mine, too. Chris went on to hunt Sunny for a decade on western roosters, and the little yellow Lab was a hard-charging trooper until the end.

I grew up with a golden retriever, so I've always had a soft spot for the breed, although my hunting over them has been limited. They're beautiful and extremely intelligent, and despite the fact that their thick coats are a big disadvantage in burr country, they're one of the more popular breeds in the country. But that popularity has come at a price: goldens have been house pets for so long that many of them have lost their drive to hunt (although their drive to retrieve doesn't seem

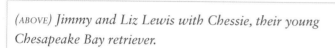

(ABOVE) *Jimmy and Liz Lewis with Chessie, their young Chesapeake Bay retriever.*

(RIGHT) *Jarod Highberg and Winsor, a yellow Labrador retriever, with the first rooster of the season.*

to have lessened one iota). There are good, hunting-stock goldens out there, but again, if I were to buy one, I'd be certain I watched one or both of the parents hunt. Don't be swayed by a list of titles following any dog's name; watch it hunt for yourself. Remember, this is an animal you'll be spending the next ten or twelve years with. It's absolutely important to find a good match.

Chesapeakes? I've hunted over one or two, and, like most of the Labs I've seen, they got the job done in a thorough, methodical manner. A Chessie's sheer size and strength is impressive, though. If you'll be hunting extremely dense cover, they might be a good dog to try. It's hard to imagine anything a Chessie couldn't bull his way through. On the other hand, if you plan to hunt hard all day long, their bulk is a disadvantage. Like long-distance runners, dogs that can hunt all day are typically lean and rangy in build. For an all-day hunter, I'd go with a smaller, lighter dog from one of the other retriever or spaniel breeds.

Both spaniels and retrievers need to be taught to quarter before the gun, if only so they can eventually ignore a rigid quartering pattern and hunt to objectives. Sound contradictory? Let me explain.

Since retrievers *must* flush birds within range, teaching them to quarter within a reasonable distance, say, twenty yards to either side and ten to twenty yards to the front, is important. But once a dog is trained to hunt within comfortable range (comfortable for you, not him), he'll engrave that distance upon his mental template, and—theoretically, at least—remain within those boundaries when he hunts. Then, gradually, you can loosen the reins and let *him* figure out where the birds are. If he's been trained well, he'll find them—and stay within range of the gun, too.

If that sounds a little like what pointers do, you're correct. Which leads us to the final category of pheasant dogs...

49

(TOP) *Goose Creek Rose, a pointing black Lab, sits at heel with a Kansas rooster.*

(BOTTOM) *Goose Creek Jake, a yellow Lab, points with style and intensity.*

Pointers

For some reason, many people think pointers aren't any "good" on pheasants. They couldn't be more wrong. German shorthairs (GSP's) have won innumerable pheasant-hunting contests (on penned birds, of course, but still), and Brittanies—perhaps the most popular pointing breed in the country—can find roosters with the best of them. Setters, English pointers, wirehairs, griffons, and other breeds all have their fans. All can be force broken to retrieve, and should be—even GSP's, wirehairs and griffons, which are the strongest retrievers of the bunch.

There's a learning curve that most pointers go through when they're learning to trail roosters, but some dogs are quicker than others. A couple of years ago, for example, I was hunting with a good friend on his uncle's ranch. Although there were pheasants all over that place, I was a bit concerned how my English setter, Rabbit, would handle them. But she seemed to have no problem switching from the relatively stationary coveys of Huns she'd cut her teeth on to the wide-open, run-till-your-tongue-hangs-out pheasants we were hunting that day

In one slough filled with reed canary grass and cattails, she pointed two or three birds, creeping, trailing, and pinning each one like a pro. But her crowning achievement came late in the day, when we combed a pasture bisected by a tiny, frozen creek bed. Fifteen minutes into our push upstream, Rabbit locked up on the edge of the bank, her butt and tail high in the air, her head almost hidden below the bank's lip. I walked up and booted a rooster out of the ankle-high grass below me.

It should have been an easy shot, but I didn't swing through and hit the bird too far back. It cartwheeled to the earth thirty yards away and immediately sprang to its feet, ready to make a run for it. I was worried— Rabbit had never retrieved a wounded rooster and they can be a nasty mouthful

Purdey points a cock pheasant in the lower right of the photo. Purdey, a Brittany, is a pheasant specialist who handles pheasants really well. Consequently she never was a top-notch Hungarian partridge dog.

for an inexperienced dog. Then, out of the corner of my eye, I spied a black and white blur rocketing past, and the next thing I knew the little dog hit that rooster like a freight train. The two of them rolled over and over in the grass and snow, but when the dust settled, she emerged triumphant with the still very-much-alive pheasant in her mouth.

Pointers require a different mind set than either retrievers or spaniels. Since their job is to find and hold game rather than flush it, they have a considerably larger playing field on which to operate. But dogs that range way out there make nervous Nellies out of many hunters. In open country, I have no problem with my setter or Brittany working at two- or three-hundred yards, a range also common to some of the GSP's I've hunted over, another excellent breed (in fact, one of the best). That said, though, both of my dogs shorten up considerably in thick cover, although I always put beeper collars or bells on them when I'm gunning for roosters. Still, if you're looking

(LEFT) Sully, Brad Ehrnman's English setter, nails a rooster in CRP. It is obvious that Sully has a nose full of hot scent.

(RIGHT) Liz Lewis moves up on Blixen, a German shorthair pointer on point.

(PREVIOUS PAGE) Lucy, Craig Janssen's Gordon setter, delivers a cock bird to hand.

for a pointer that tends to hunt close, I'd suggest giving the continentals—wirehairs and griffons—a serious look. Both breeds tend to work close to the

General, an older German wirehair pointer, holds a retrieved rooster at Sandanona Pheasantry in Millbrook, New York.

gun and both have excellent noses—in fact, a friend's griffon has placed in a number of our local NSTRA trials, beating out any number of pointers, setters, and Brittanies, despite the fact that the faster dogs are halfway across the course by the time the wirehairs are just building up a good head of steam. The truth is, a very fast dog can be a disadvantage in the thick cover pheasants love.

It's just as important to stay with a pointer that is making game as it is to stay with any of the flushing breeds. Pheasants are pheasants, after all, and they're nothing if not moving targets. Yes, your pointer will try to pin a running rooster—that's his job—but there's no guarantee he'll be able to hold him forever, so get to your dog as quickly as it is prudent and safe to do so.

Finally, there are some who think pheasants will ruin a good pointer. That *may* be true if a dog is judged solely by his performance in a field trial, but under actual hunting conditions I've never seen that happen. In the real world, the world of wild pheasants on wild land, the birds get to lay down the ground rules. My dogs invariably trail, creep, and break point on running roosters, but rarely resort to that behavior on more mannered gamebirds like bobwhite quail. And if they do slip up once in a while and bust a bird, well…I remember all the pheasants I've missed after flawless dog work and that puts everything else in perspective.

(ABOVE) *Howard Davis walks in on a double point by Ruby, an English pointer, and Sam, his tricolor setter. Both are backed by Annie, his orange Belton setter.*

(LEFT) *Datus Proper, author of* Pheasants of the Mind, *walks past Huckleberry, a liver-colored German shorthair that is pointing an early season pheasant.*

(ABOVE) *Gretchen, a German shorthair, chases a winged rooster in a stubble field.*

(LEFT) *Loving it: Purdey being patted by Michael McIntosh.*

(PREVIOUS PAGE) *Whoopie, we're going hunting! Brittany Purdey dances around Brian Ramsey at the commencement of a hunt. Both are young and beside themselves with joy.*

Guns & Shooting

Ron Spomer

W HEN CHOOSING A PHEASANT GUN REMEMBER TWO THINGS: 1. They all work. 2. Some work better than others.

For decades the 12-gauge throwing magnum quantities of No. 6, No. 5 or No. 4 shot—the harder the better—has been glorified as the ideal rooster buster. This has contributed to poor shooting, frustration and even pain because not everyone is built to handle a big twelve throwing heavy charges. A more efficient prescription would match the individual to the gun. Better to dispense a smaller number of pellets on target than double that number into the wild blue yonder.

This doesn't mean the 12-gauge is wrong. In the right hands it may indeed be the ultimate ringneck terminator. All else being equal, 1¼-ounces of shot has the potential for making more hits than does one ounce of pellets. "All else," then, is the key, and the handle to that key is gun fit.

In order for a shotgun to perform as intended, the shooter must be able to maneuver it in line with his vision and maintain that sight picture until the gun fires. The gun essentially becomes an extension of the shooter's body. It should point as naturally, easily and accurately as his finger. Where his eye looks, his barrel points. This requires the gun both fit the shooter's shape (neck length, arm length, cheek height, etc.) and be light enough so the shooter can bring it into battery quickly, but not so light that he flinches in anticipation of its recoil.

> *Better to dispense a smaller number of pellets on target than double that number in the wild blue yonder.*

(BELOW) *A profusely engraved Krieghoff 12-gauge with gold inlays of a setter and flushing pheasants.*

(OPPOSITE PAGE) *A 20-gauge Grulla No. 2 sidelock double-barrel shotgun and a beautiful Nebraska cock bird. This gun is unique because it is has two forearms, one splinter and one semi-beavertail, and two sets of ventilated ribbed barrels.*

In Montana, Will Brewster moves up on Jessie, a tricolor setter. Gasper Accardi of Lagrangeville, New York, bred Jessie as a ruffed grouse dog. She had the best nose of any dog the photographer has ever seen.

According to physicists, for every action there is an opposite and equal reaction. In the case of a 7-pound, 12-gauge shotgun spitting 1¼-ounces of shot at 1,260 fps, that opposite reaction amounts to 32.7 foot-pounds (ft. lbs.) of free recoil (the force of the gun jumping back in reaction to the shot.) Just how violent this feels to each shooter varies. Some hardly notice, some flinch badly. Adding a pound to the gun reduces recoil to 28.8 ft. lbs. Reducing the charge of shot to 1⅛-ounce and the velocity to 1,200 fps drops recoil to 23.3 ft. lbs.

In contrast, 1-ounce loads at 1,220 fps from a 6-pound 20-gauge generate just 22.4 ft. lbs. of "kick," suggesting you can carry a lighter gun without suffering a painful belt in the shoulder. Of course, you'll be throwing fewer pellets at your birds, but if the gun patterns evenly, mounts and fits properly and you shoot it well, you'll get your birds.

Contrary to popular dogma, a good shooter using a proper fitting 28-gauge can kill pheasants dead-as-a-hammer out to 35 yards. In short, it's not the size of the gun or shell so much as the effectiveness of the operator.

This might be the place to dispel a myth. Large gauges and magnum shotshells do not necessarily "hit harder" than smaller gauges or standard shotshells. Many magnum shells actually launch at lower velocities than standard rounds. Since a 6-shot pellet weighs the same regardless which gauge it's fired from, muzzle velocity determines how much "sting" or energy it will carry. An ounce of 6s from a 20-gauge at 1,400 fps will hit harder at 40 yards than 1½ ounces of 6s from a 12-gauge at 1,100 fps. Velocity and pellet size determine how much energy a pellet carries downrange. However, it is also true that the 335 No. 6 pellets in a magnum 12-gauge load are a whole lot more than the 225 pellets in a 20-gauge load. If more of these pellets strike the target, more total energy will be delivered and the magnum load will, indeed, "hit harder." Unfortunately, not all shotguns pattern magnum charges of shot well, and this is the crux of the issue: evenly distributed pellets (the pattern) delivered on target determine a shotgun's effectiveness.

So where does this leave the man or woman trying to select the proper shotgun? In the driver's seat. Don't feel that you must purchase a heavy 12-gauge in order to be a deadly pheasant shot. On average, figure 5-yards-less-effective range for each size down in gauge, all else being equal. If a 10-

gauge throws a sufficiently dense pattern at 50 yards, a 12-gauge with the same choke and patterning ability should be equally effective at 45 yards, a 16-gauge at 40-yards, 20-gauge at 35 yards and 28-gauge at 30 yards. Even the lowly .410 bore can be a pheasant gun in the right hands at 20 yards, though that narrow bore's inability to efficiently handle pellets larger than 7½ limit its application for ringnecks. Regardless the gauge, different choke/ammunition combinations can extend or shorten effective distances. Yes, a tightly choked 12- or 10-gauge may shoot deadly patterns at 50 yards, but you'll have to manhandle the bulky, heavy launch platform over hill and dale. In addition you'll have to perfect the difficult task of putting those pellets on target at such extreme range plus give up opportunities at closer flushing birds. Most pheasants are shot closer to 20 yards than 50 anyway. The key is to buy a shotgun that fits properly, feels lively and patterns evenly. Just remember this: the heavier the shot charge and the lighter the gun, the heavier the recoil.

Double Barrel Break Action

This category includes both side-by-side doubles, the classic upland guns of the late 19th and early 20th century, and over/under doubles. Side-by-sides fell from favor after W.W. II because they were more expensive to build than pumps and autoloaders. In addition, America was having a love affair with mechanized efficiency and firepower. By the 1970s, however, the rising popularity of over/under double barrels at skeet and trap ranges began to leak onto the hunting fields and change the tide.

Today over/unders are the hot sellers. Additionally, bird numbers were dropping and shooting opportunities dwindling at the same time sportsmen's affluence was growing. A philosophical shift in attitudes placed more importance on the hunt and its accouterments than on large bags. Given limited opportunities to hunt and even fewer chances to shoot at game, sportsmen and women wanted to heighten their appreciation of the entire experience by using a good-looking, sleek, quick handling gun, and the over/under was it.

In the last five years this paradigm shift has led to a resurgence in side-by-side doubles and even side-by-sides with external hammers. Regardless how the barrels are stacked, double guns are ideal tools for pheasant hunting. Because each barrel wears a different choke, a hunter is instantly ready for close or distant flushes. Screw-in chokes make it possible to tune the gun for nearly any shooting condition. It's the ultimate in versatility. Double guns break down into three compact pieces for easy

A 16-gauge, pre-war, Charles Daly over/under leans against a fence. The 16 gauge is perfect for pheasants.

cleaning, transport and safe storage, too. Because most of their working parts are contained within the action walls and grip, they remain clean for years. Malfunctions are rare.

(ABOVE) Scott Wuebber flushes a cock pheasant on a beautiful fall morning in Montana.

(RIGHT) Jerry Robinson shoots an Auto 5 Belgium Browning.

Autoloader

The autoloading action shotgun has been around since John Browning engineered the A-5 "humpback" just before the 20th century. The first models hit stores in 1900. Autos don't have the style and cache of doubles or even the blue-collar chutzpah of pumps, but they tame recoil better than all the rest by spreading out the jolt as the recoil energy moves the bolt back to cycle a fresh round into battery. Dozens of companies build autos using proven gas and inertia recoil systems. Most are rugged and dependable. Many are nicely balanced and trim. All can prove deadly in the field. Because their bolts need to slide back far enough to pick up another shell from the magazine, they are longer than double barrels with equal barrel lengths. This means you get roughly the same sighting plane with a 24-inch barreled auto as a 28-inch barreled double. The swing-through or follow through momentum of the shorter-barreled auto might not be quite the same, but it's close.

Autos don't break down into so handy a package as doubles, but barrels screw off easily. Removal of bolts, springs, magazine followers and other parts isn't all that complicated or difficult either. After

a few dismantling operations, cleaning becomes fairly quick and easy, and that is enough to keep most autos shooting smoothly and consistently season after season. Autos are ideal for small shooters or the recoil shy. Screw-in chokes increase versatility, but you can only use one at a time.

Pump-Action

The old shell-shucker was as common as fence posts in post-war America. Everyone from Farmer John to trap champions and trick shooters used them. They were and remain rugged, durable, fast, and effective. Like an old plow horse they'll trudge through the worst of it while high-spirited autoloaders balk. You're more likely to drag an inexpensive pump than a high-dollar double through Dakota snow, Iowa rain, and Kansas dust. Most are built with inexpensive walnut, birch, or synthetic stocks so you won't cringe when they're scratched. A pump won't spread recoil the way an auto will, but a fast hand can cycle them faster than the fastest auto. That's been proven. Barrels are easily screwed off and entire trigger units can be easily removed for thorough cleaning. The camming action of the pump lets you chamber dirty or slightly over-sized shells that an auto might refuse. Despite their ungainly look, pumps can feel downright sprightly and handle nicely. They offer the best dollar value of any repeater.

Single-Shots

Usually reserved for starter guns, single-shots come in two action types: break-action with exposed hammer and bolt-action. I don't believe anyone manufactures a bolt-action single-shot scattergun anymore, but a number are available on the used market. Several companies still make new break-actions. Because the break-action must be hand-loaded one shell at a time, can be carried broken open, and must have its external hammer pulled back before firing, it is considered an extremely safe firearm for novices. I agree except for that outside hammer. It is often so heavy that young thumbs slip before pulling it back to full cock. The hammer flies forward and discharges the gun prematurely. Modern break-actions are built with transverse-bar safeties that interrupt this premature release, but watch out with old models. Given a choice, I'd outfit a new shooter with a modern double and allow him to load but one shell at a time, then carry it with the safety on.

Barrels and Chokes

The shorter a barrel the more quickly it points. The longer a barrel the more easily it "carries through" a swing. In most pheasant shooting, a smooth, consistent follow through is required more often than a quick poke. After more than 35 years of hunting pheasants with barrels from 22 to 32 inches, I vote heartily for the 28-inch tube as the all-round best. I could agree to a 30-inch stretcher for long-range shooting and pass shooting and a 26-inch stub for brushier habitats, but I see no need to go shorter or longer. Longer barrels will not shoot harder nor reach farther. Not enough to notice outside a ballistic lab, anyway.

As for chokes, most pheasant gunners overdo it. The idea of full-choke for ringnecks was born well over 75 years ago when ammunition was inefficient. Soft lead pellets rubbed themselves flat against steel barrels and planed wildly in the wind. The plastic shot sleeve solved most of that. Harder lead shot, buffered copper-plated shot, steel shot, tungsten shot, and now super-heavy shot pattern much more tightly than old soft lead pellets. The upshot is that a modern shell will generally throw a full-choke pattern through a modified choke, a modified pattern through an improved cylinder tube. Exacerbating

Six roosters and a 20-gauge Model 12 Winchester with a straight English stock and rather nice wood.

this is one's tendency to over-estimate range. That last cock you swore you hit at 35 yards was probably closer to 27 yards. Count steps to your birds and you'll soon realize how close most of them are when hit. All of this suggested to me years ago that a cylinder choke and improved cylinder choke were ideal for 80 percent of my pheasant work. On windy days or during late season hunts when roosters consistently flush wild I might step up to a modified. I haven't felt the need for a full-choke in 30 years. If you're still using tight chokes, open up and see the difference.

Ammunition

The three most popular pellet sizes for ringnecks are No. 6, No. 5 and No. 4. I'll employ No. 7½ on early birds and even late ones flushing close. The smaller pellets produce denser patterns, but they shed energy quickly and fail to penetrate deeply enough at longer ranges. This is why No. 6 shot is nearly perfect. Reserve No. 4s for long-range, late-season birds. No. 5 is an ideal compromise anytime and is now widely available in the Pheasant Forever-Federal "Wing-Shok" shells. Smaller gauges pattern best with smaller shot. The 28-gauge rarely patterns well with anything larger than No. 6, and No. 7½ almost always pattern better. The 20-gauge handles No. 6s beautifully, but No. 4s are often too large to flow smoothly through that narrow bore. Once you've moved up to a 16-gauge you can handle any reasonable pheasant pellet. Heavy charges of shot, regardless of pellet size, also reach a point of diminishing returns in various gauges. Many hunters discover they shoot better and bag more birds with fast 1⅛-ounce shells instead of 1¼- or 1½-ounce payloads

(LEFT) *A spent shell being removed from a Parker VHE side-by-side.*

(RIGHT) *Winsor, a yellow Lab, waits in the truck above a wooden Winchester Super X shell box.*

in 12-gauge guns. The $1^1/_{16}$-ounce load is optimum in the 16-gauge, the 1-ounce in the 20-gauge and the ¾-ounce in the 28-gauge.

Scott Wuebber admires a late-season, long-tailed rooster that he took with a 20-gauge Remington Model 1100 Automatic.

An effective option these days is any of the new light-charge, high-speed shells. By reducing payload weight and increasing powder capacity, manufacturers are building hard-hitting shells that compensate for one of the most common shooting mistakes—insufficient lead. A 1-ounce swarm of shot streaking out at 1,400 fps may stop more pheasants for you than a 1¼-ounce charge stepping out at a more sedate 1,250 fps. The lighter load should recoil less, too.

Ideally you should pattern various shells/shot sizes and chokes to determine which produces evenly spaced patterns through which no pheasant could fit without being struck by at least 8 pellets. Three or four will often do the job, but because not all pellets reach a flying target at the same time (pellets string out, some traveling faster than others) some of the 8 pellets that strike your pattern board won't reach a real pheasant before he's flown by.

One can nit-pick guns and loads ad infinitum, which makes interesting and sometimes heated camp conversation but rarely leads to more birds in the bag. Focus on selecting an action-type you enjoy, then select a gun weight and balance that feels sprightly and natural in your hands. Have a professional (usually a gunsmith or shotgun shooting coach) check it for proper fit, and pattern various loads/chokes through it to find which combination your gun shoots best. Then go pheasant hunting. That's the best part.

Pheasant hunter's dream: a big flush of pheasants at Tumbleweed Lodge in Harrold, South Dakota. More than 150 pheasants flushed from a two-acre field behind the lodge.

Three Seasons in One

Ron Spomer

ACCORDING TO ORNITHOLOGISTS, PHEASANTS NEVER METAMORPHOSE into different species. According to hunters, they sure seem to. Over the course of a season, roosters transmogrify from approachable, accommodating, close flushers on opening day into ultra-spooky, long-distance sprinters by mid-season. After a big snowfall they change again, holding tight like October quail. By late season they coalesce into large flocks that flush as wild as snow geese. This avian multiple-personality-disorder mandates flexibility in hunting strategy.

Early Season

Some hard-core ringneck chasers consider opening-week roosters beneath their dignity. Too easy. Not so pointing dog owners. They welcome the chance to work their four-legged partners on a pheasant that will actually stay in

> *Pheasants wise up and change behavior quickly—sometimes in a matter of hours rather than days.*

one place long enough to be pointed. Credit youthful inexperience for such cooperative behavior. Depending on the success of the spring hatch, upwards of 90 percent of opening-day cocks may be tender, almost trusting, four-month-old rookies. Fine eating, but not much of a sporting challenge. Virtually any hunter just stumbling through reasonable pheasant cover can bag a few opening-day birds—if he can find a place to hunt.

After a long spring and summer layoff, most upland hunters are so eager to take the field that they choke public lands. At some popular wildlife management areas you have to arrive hours before the opening bell to garner a spot. And if you haven't reserved a seat on private land, you're too late to join that show. Don't waste your time driving door-to-door, hat in hand. The message is simple: plan ahead. You should contact landowners and schedule your hunt months, sometimes years ahead of time.

If you're shy or prefer hunting public land, scout before opening day and plot your line of march based on habitat and standard pheasant behavior. Traditionally cover is abundant at the start of the season and young birds are feasting on insects as much as grain. They like to roost overnight in expansive grass fields and move to feeding areas at sunrise, avoiding thick vegetation if it is wet with dew. If undisturbed they walk, forage and preen in mowed grass, alfalfa, and wheat

(LEFT) Rose the Nose ("Rosie") works a running pheasant that she pinned at the end of the cover next to a field. Her tail and body language say she is birdy.

stubble or sit atop hay stacks until ground cover dries. By late morning they've shifted to secure roosting sites, usually tall cover that is fairly open at ground level—like standing corn or sunflowers. Here they can run to escape four-legged predators

Kevin Haight pulls up on a rooster that flushed from a milo field as Charlie, a black Lab belonging to Ms. Terry Regan, sits to the flush.

and hide from airborne attackers. In late afternoon they again move into feeding areas before hiking or flying back to nocturnal roosts at sundown.

Keep these behaviors and habitats in mind while hunting, but understand that other hunters will disrupt the birds' routine. A sensible plan might be to begin searching grass roosting fields at sunrise, then walking standing corn through mid-day. While you do, watch where other hunters work and where flushed birds land. Go after them. Hunters and dogs often force pheasants into cover they wouldn't normally use during early season, such as cattail sloughs, dense weeds, even woodlands. At least twice over the years I've found opening-day roosters hiding in plowed fields. Don't be afraid to modify your plan of attack.

If you arrive late to the ball or don't wish to race others to the coverts, don't despair. While everyone else rushes through the cover, hang back and watch where disturbed birds fly. Note which coverts are bypassed or hit lightly. Then move in behind your competition. Hunt methodically and slowly, knowing that inexperienced birds are confused and likely to stick tight to cover. Allow your dog plenty of time to scour for scent. Stop frequently for several minutes to unnerve sitting birds. Move erratically rather than in a straight line.

Mid-Season

Where early season pheasants are pursued aggressively and often, they wise up and change behavior quickly—sometimes in a matter of hours

Dan Groshens swings on a big rooster pinned by a Brittany.

rather than days. When you begin noticing wild flushes, or when your dog begins trailing scent for long distances, assume you're hunting mid-season birds. You don't just walk-up these feathered marathoners; you outsmart and outflank them. Because cover is still tall, dense and abundant, roosters have countless options for escape. You'll need advanced planning, coordination, and precision attack to intercept them. Your most valuable resource now becomes information, specifically where birds are hiding. This is almost always where they are least disturbed. Human nature being what it is, hunters predictably walk the same fields and brush pockets from the same directions. In doing so they train roosters where, when and how to escape. The birds congregate where they are least harassed. Often this is land posted against trespass. Sometimes it's inconvenient or isolated cover such as islands or small patches of weeds far out in otherwise barren fields. Sometimes it's an unlikely hiding spot such as a shelterbelt or weedy vegetable garden beside a busy farmstead. Sometimes it is deep, miserable cover no one wants to wallow through, such as briar thickets or cattail wetlands. (You don't know misery until you've walked through a cloud of cattail down. It swirls up your nose and plasters onto your eyelids as you suck it down your throat. Plunge ahead to escape and you shake more of it loose. When you finally stop to let it settle, eyes scrunched tight, hand over your nose and mouth, a rooster will flush at your feet. Pheasants love cattail down.)

Pheasants find intimidating hiding places quickly. Mark Kayser and I once stomped hundreds of acres of prime, tall-grass public hunting fields in western South Dakota, but flushed just three hens and one rooster. Assuming we weren't the first to work those grasslands, we secured permission to hunt a bordering private field of cut corn that no self-respecting pheasant would have stayed in past breakfast time. A rattlesnake would have had trouble hiding in that cover. As anticipated, we moved but a handful of birds, and all out of range—until we came to a pocket of tall kochia weeds no larger than a basketball court. It erupted in feathers. We were too busy shooting to get an accurate count, but at least 50 roosters flushed from that insignificant speck of cover. Undoubtedly, no one had disturbed it for days. It pays to knock on doors and gain permission to hunt private fields near public hunting areas during mid-season.

As a general rule, hunt mid-season cover "against-the-grain." If the obvious approach is from the road, come in from the other end of the field, even if it means hiking a half-mile of barren pasture to get there. If a brushy fence line and a mowed grass strip connect a grain field with a grassy roost field, walk the mowed grass. When hunting with a partner or two, plan ambushes. Let one gunner sneak into position along an obvious escape line before the other works the roosting cover with a dog. If you don't have a large party to pull off a mass sweep of a big grain field, let one or two blockers hide in the field's far corners while one with a dog zig zags through the middle. Hunt as quietly as possible to confuse quarry used to keeping track of two-legged predators via slamming doors, whistling, and shouting.

Don't let big fields of cover discourage you. A single hunter can roust roosters from a huge CRP field by working its edges corner to corner. Expect flushes near the corners. Once you've circumnavigated the field, cut diagonally across it and be ready for the mother load. If you still need a

A rooster holds tight. Pheasants often hold tight allowing hunters to walk by them.

(ABOVE) *A cock pheasant on a dead run through CRP.*

(LEFT) *A black Labrador retriever makes a high-head and high-tailed retrieve.*

bird or two, head toward the landing site of the biggest bunch and resume working toward the corners. Pheasants often remain in a big field if only one or two hunters work it. Recently brother

Hunting a huge CRP field in North Dakota late in the day.

Bob and I hunted a vast CRP field on Richard Kieffer's farm near White Lake, South Dakota, late in the year. The wind was up and so were the pheasants, flushing hundreds of yards ahead. Undaunted, we followed, again pushing birds up wild. This time many circled back and landed behind us, virtually in the same spot from which they'd initially flushed. Back we went. Up they went, but now a few were holding tight and the dogs began nosing them up inside 20-gauge range. We got 'em.

Late Season

After the challenge of mid-season, many hunters are ready to give up, which is their loss. Late-season hunting can be deeply satisfying and surprisingly productive. Satisfaction results from persevering against difficult conditions, enjoying the open spaces with minimum competition, and finding birds where others have failed. Yes, pheasant numbers have been reduced significantly but so has cover. By the time the calendar flips past Thanksgiving, most crops have been harvested, many fields have been plowed, leaves have fallen, and frosts have toppled many weeds. Crushing snows may have flattened tall-grass fields. Surviving birds are forced to concentrate in remaining cattail and bulrush sloughs, CRP grass fields, woody brush thickets, odd weed patches, and shelterbelts. Such collections of birds are a double-edged sword: they are easy to locate but often difficult to approach. The flightiest bird in the bunch flushes at the first hint of trouble and that sets off a chain reaction. Within seconds every pheasant in a 100-acre field has fled. I've watched waves of pheasants leapfrog one another down the length of a CRP field by the hundreds. Such numbers are encouraging, but how do you get close enough to invite any to an intimate dinner?

Again, stealth and an unconventional approach are productive. Avoid the obvious routes, hunt quietly, and push cover toward traps, which can be even denser cover in which birds might feel safe enough to hold or barren fields into which birds do not wish to expose themselves. Whenever possible, post a hunter at bottlenecks and escape points. Posters should sneak into position and

Roger Keckeissen is about to shoot a late season trophy rooster that was pinned by his setter, Sam, on the edge of a creek bottom.

hide if possible. They'll often hear birds running through cover or see them sneaking past. Those are the times to jump up and yell "Surprise!"

Late-season pheasants fall into ruts, especially if left undisturbed for several days. From nocturnal roosting sites in grass fields or wetland vegetation, they'll walk or fly as necessary to the nearest feeding site, usually a harvested grain field. Here they fill up quickly and rush back to protective cover, preferably tall overstory with ground cover open enough for easy running. Shelterbelts, brush thickets, cattail sloughs, wild sunflowers, and stands of kochia weeds are prime spots. An hour or two before sundown they again move to feeding sites, fill their crops, and zip back into bedding cover. The return is often late, hasty, and on the wing, making pass shooting a distinct possibility. Scout flight paths with binoculars and move under the flight path early the next afternoon. Hide in a ditch or behind cover until the birds are in range before standing to shoot.

When working cover with or without dogs, expect everything from running birds and wild flushes to holding birds and boot-lace flushes. Veteran cocks know all the tricks and don't hesitate to try them. You should do the same. As during mid-season, work dense cover toward bottlenecks and openings, field corners, and dense holding cover. Trust your dog and follow where his nose leads. It isn't unusual to trail a running ringneck for a mile before cornering it. When flocks flush wild, follow them up quickly and keep pressure on them. After two or three flushes, battalion unity often breaks down. Individual birds sneak off, stick tight, or otherwise compromise themselves. Be ready at all times. Expect flushes behind you. When approaching tall cover, anticipate flushes out the back side. Two or three hunters are always more effective than one because of this. Where huge flocks regularly abandon cover en masse at long range, try to surround them before moving in. Mike Weathermon and I did this on his family ranch near Winner, South Dakota, one December. The previous day we'd chased a big band of birds that wouldn't let us get within scattergun range. On the second day I sneaked into a low draw running through the center of their CRP escape field while Mike circled to the northwest corner. When he began walking southeast toward me, the ringneck ringleader sounded the alarm and the field began to empty, many of the fliers passing near me. A pair of rusty, long-tailed roosters didn't make it.

If you face a large field with multiple escape routes and insufficient man-power to cover all of them, set out a few blaze-orange dummies. A jacket, vest, or simply a cap on

A big rooster walks through the snow. Roosters that make it to the season's end are ultimate survivalists and have gained trophy status.

(LEFT) *Flying Falcon Drake stretched out and flying across the snow in pursuit of a fallen bird. Who says goldens do not have a lot of go?*

(RIGHT) *Pheasant tracks in freshly fallen snow.*

a fence post will spook birds, encouraging them to run or fly a safer-looking path—perhaps the one under which you are hiding. If you feel the need to augment this subterfuge, hang a portable radio or CD player with the scarecrow garment. The sound will nudge birds away from quite a distance.

Snow can work with or against a two-legged hunter. If deep and fluffy, it often prevents avian running, forcing birds to hold or fly. They usually choose to hold. One November John Cardarelli turned his excellent setters loose in central South Dakota after an overnight snowfall of 18 inches. It was so fluffy that pheasants actually scuttled underneath it while the dogs plowed and bounded through until pointing the hidden treasures. We'd kick under the snow until a bird burst up like a missile launched from a submarine. When missed roosters landed, they often stayed put. The dogs would point, we'd peek into the landing hole, see dark tail feathers and kick out the gift. Sadly, it was all too easy and we were done within the hour.

Heavy, drifted snow with a thin crust allows birds to run while we and our dogs often sink to our knees. Under these exhausting conditions scouting and planning are crucial. You must isolate and surround birds unless you use cross-country skis to chase them down. Sometimes it's worth the trouble to find a snowmobile in order to reach distant coverts where pheasants have congregated. Few hunters will walk through deep snow to reach such places. Once wind packs snow, as it often does in the Plains States, the landscape becomes the equivalent of a barren field. You're back to working pocket cover, the thicker the better.

Twenty years ago the late season was largely unloved and unhunted by the masses, but that has changed as sportsmen have attempted to avoid early season crowds and access private land. Now only extreme cold or deep snow keeps hunters at bay. Nevertheless, late season can be productive, and it's always invigorating.

Early, late, or in between, pheasants and pheasant hunting remains an ever-changing challenge—exactly what a real hunter wants. Use your head as well as your legs, persist, and enjoy the second-best recreation this planet offers.

"Upland bird restoration: The time is now."

Mark Herwig

From those simple words, a headline in a Minnesota newspaper story, would spring a grassroots, nationwide upland conservation movement that is today's Pheasants Forever.

Those seven simple words comprised the headline to an article written by Dennis Anderson, outdoor editor for the St. Paul Pioneer Press and Dispatch. In that first, emotional article March 7, 1982 Anderson did not mix his words. "Up until now, we've done little but complain. Until now we've stood by, watching Minnesota's native habitat disappear, and with it wildlife of all types. Instead of doing something, we've come to accept our present situation as inevitable and tolerable.

"It was inevitable that marshes would be drained, we say to ourselves. It was inevitable that ditches would be burned. It was inevitable that fields would be plowed each fall, leaving no winter cover for upland birds. And because it was inevitable, it's now tolerable. We tolerate winters such as these, when hens and roosters freeze to death, their faces mere clumps of ice after they turn windward to a final, desperate attempt to survive.

"Have you ever watched a pheasant freeze?"

A thinking, feeling person could not ignore Anderson's words. He made us look at ourselves, pushing us to not only take responsibility for the disease, but the cure as well.

"They're not pretty sights, " he continued, "these effects of high per-acre yields and bottom-line profitability....Nor are they the stuff of award ceremonies, the stuff that makes man proud."

Anderson's fire and brimstone then softened into a plea for action. He went on to cite the example of the state of

(LEFT) *Good habitat benefits all types of wildlife. Vegetation between fence lines provides shelter next to a western grain field.*

(RIGHT) *A Pheasants Forever project sign. The long-tailed bird has made a tremendous comeback in the Midwest and West due to CRP and P.F. Pheasants Forever and its volunteers have made and continue to make a big difference.*

Pheasants Forever volunteers work at a grassroots level creating and enhancing wildlife habitat. Photos by Mark Herwig/ Pheasants Forever.

South Dakota's successful pheasant restoration program, insisting Minnesotans could do much the same if only we cared enough to try.

"So it's up to those of us who are willing. …The birds need your help. Write me … tell me what you think about the restoration idea."

And write they did. In a March 21, 1982 article Anderson wrote, "A lot has happened since I wrote two weeks ago about the need for a Minnesota upland bird restoration program." He reported over 100 people wrote him and another 50 called. Anderson printed the names of everyone who wrote in, as well as many of their letters. Most were simple hunters from all corners of the state, people who cared very much about the future of habitat, pheasants and hunting.

Anderson, using the bully pulpit of his large, state-wide daily newspaper, then called for a pheasant stamp to pay farmers to manage marginal acres for pheasant habitat. Sound familiar? It should—today PF is renowned for working with private landowners. The policy was also a hint of things to come in the form of the federal Conservation Reserve Program—a 39-million acre grassland conservation initiative many credit PF with continuing and expanding.

A little later in the article, Anderson introduces the name of Pheasants Forever for the first time.

"We've formed a group called Pheasants Forever. At first, the organization will work in Minnesota. In the future, chapters may be formed in other states." PF now has chapters in 28 states, members in all other states and chapters in our sister organization PF-Canada.

PF's first goal was passing the Minnesota pheasant stamp, but beyond that, Anderson said PF would, "work to ensure that a healthy population of pheasants has a home in Minnesota Forever. To do this, Pheasants Forever will work with, and—with luck—eventually employ wildlife biologists." PF now has 21 wildlife biologists around the country and a growing cadre of Habitat Team specialists in three states.

"I've come to realize," Anderson wrote in his March 21st column, "that we, each of us, have the opportunity to make a difference, and for the better. I think the low water mark on habitat loss has finally been reached. Pheasants and other upland birds now have friends who, together, will ensure their well being. It'll be a while before Pheasants Forever is ready to accept memberships. So please, don't send money. But stay tuned. It won't be long." PF now has over 100,000 members.

A Pheasants Forever dinner in Sigourney, Iowa. Dinners are Pheasants Forever primary source of income with 100 percent of the money raised by the chapters remaining with the chapters for local projects. There are more than 550 PF chapters in the United States and Canada.

Baby steps

In PF's first publication entitled "Rooster Tales," dated February 1983, the organization urged its 500 members to first push for passage of the Minnesota Pheasant Stamp. The newsletter, forerunner of today's Pheasants Forever Journal, then ponders PF's first baby steps into an unknown future.

"The board realizes that, as the organization grows and chapters are established in outstate Minnesota, the organization will need a responsible, part-time person to oversee, guide and inspire the day-to-day activities....In sum, the board's immediate goals are to pass the pheasant stamp and to hold a successful banquet-fundraiser."

The first banquet

A little over a year after Anderson's ground breaking column calling for pheasant restoration, the fledgling Pheasants Forever held its first banquet on April 15, 1983. By now, Anderson had another believer on his team, his co-worker and St. Paul Pioneer Press national advertising director, Jeff Finden. (Finden later became PF's first executive director, a position he served in until 2000.)

Together, Anderson, Finden and others organized that first banquet. In a Pioneer Press article by Anderson, entitled, "Pheasants Forever draws 800 to inaugural banquet," the state's hunter-conservationists first heard about the upland juggernaut that would soon sweep the nation.

"Nearly 800 sportsmen and women gathered at the Prom Center in St. Paul Friday night," the article began, "to dine on roast pheasant, celebrate the passage of the Minnesota pheasant stamp bill and raise money for Pheasants Forever, a year-old organization which has as its goal breathing new life into the state's dwindling ringneck population. The event was one of the biggest of its kind ever held in Minnesota."

The article also mentioned several early PF boosters, among them famed outdoor writer Jimmy Robinson. At the banquet, the late Robinson presented PF with two $1,000 checks; one from himself and the other from the late Twin Cities advertising magnate Robert Naegele Sr. They were PF's first Life Members.

At the banquet, attorney Robert Larson, who donated his services to ferry PF through its early legal stages, presented "1983 Conservation Awards" to PF's first business partners, Old Dutch Foods, Control Data Corp. and the St. Paul Pioneer Press and Dispatch. Larson remains Secretary of the PF national Board of Directors.

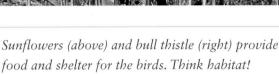
Sunflowers (above) and bull thistle (right) provide food and shelter for the birds. Think habitat!

The first banquet was a success. Over $20,000 was raised to get the organization started and start putting habitat in the ground. In the printed program of that first banquet, PF's founders struck an optimistic and prophetic tone, announcing that, **"the organization's 1,000-plus members believe they have before them an opportunity to reverse the course of wildlife history in Minnesota. It is an opportunity they seize gladly."**

The dream takes hold

Digging through a stack of dusty boxes and piles of musty newspaper clippings and office memos at Pheasants Forever headquarters in St. Paul, Minnesota, I found something quite simple, but profound in the way it reveals why Pheasants Forever has been blessed with 20 years of success.

After hunching over a large stack of tattered papers, old photos and newspapers for several hours, I came upon a pile of plain ledger paper with some dates and handwritten notes in ink. It was a sort of brief journal written by Don Lamb, one of PF's early supporters, chapter president and PF national board member from northwest Iowa.

Lamb started his notes with this simple, but telling record:

"December 1983—Had a terrible blizzard. Literally wiped the pheasants out."

He continued:

"November 1984—Went hunting. Saw two hens. It used to be the pheasants capitol of the world."

"Two weeks later—saw article about PF."

"Started chapter in January 1985."

"Started with 275 members. Raised $11 thou first banquet in 3/85"

"Planted 17,000 trees and shrubs in first year."

Lamb's simple, brief words describing the tragedy of pheasants needlessly sacrificed to a prairie blizzard, empty fields come hunting season, starting a chapter, having a banquet and planting winter cover is nothing short of the formula that has made Pheasants Forever a success.

A later journal entry speaks to the conservation ethic, patience and devotion characteristic of Pheasants Forever members:

"Not seeing a lot of results now—expect to see impact in 10-12 years."

Lamb refers to yet another major PF building block, federal legislative action, in his typical understated way: **"CRP program—have thousands of acres."**

He next comments, briefly of course, on another pillar of PF's success—partnerships.

"Really accepted well by county. Local businesses very generous—give us very valuable things—stereos, shotguns, golf clubs—for banquets. Some aren't even members."

Big blue stem, a native long-stem prairie grass, provides pheasants and other wildlife with year-round protection from avian predators and excellent winter cover. Big blue stem is easily identified by its turkey-foot-like seed head.

Phenomenal growth

I came across another stack of papers clipped together, each one entitled "Pheasants Forever chronology."

"The records, which document PF's phenomenal early growth, speak for themselves.

1982: "Membership total/year end—N/A (not applicable)."

1983: "Membership total/year end—1,000."

1984: 3,000 members   1985: 6,000 members   1986: 12,000 members

1987: 25,000 members   1988: 34,250 members   1989: 46,000 members

The historical log noted numerous PF accomplishments in Minnesota and around the country. They included ditch mowing delay campaigns and victories, state habitat funding bills, the hiring of more PF staff, state and national awards, a new seed program, PF trust funds to finance larger projects, new state private lands programs, and the 1985 Farm Bill and CRP.

On a 1986 report, there's a brief historical note about Jeff Finden, PF's co-founder and first executive director. "PF moves to a small building in White Bear Lake from Jeff Finden's basement." (PF's national headquarters remain in White Bear Lake.)

Hankster the Gangster ("Hank"), a fine English setter owned by David and Julie Kirkland, peers out of a kennel. Hank has had an abundance of birds and handles them exceptionally well. Hank is a "staunch" supporter of Pheasants Forever.

Strong leadership

Jeff Finden said he and Dennis Anderson, both passionate hunters, used to lunch together once in a while when they worked at the St. Paul Pioneer Press and Dispatch.

"That was really the beginning. We wondered why there were no pheasants, and eventually it got around to 'maybe we should start an organization to address the issue.' We knew people in the Minnesota Department of Natural Resources and started talking to them. We decided Minnesota needed a pheasant restoration program funded by a $5 habitat stamp. That was the first thing we set out to do," Finden recalled. The late Gov. Rudy Perpich signed the legislation into law at that first PF banquet in 1983.

The new Minnesota Pheasant Stamp raised $500,000/year for the birds. "We came to the realization, however, that a half million was a drop in the bucket. It wouldn't restore pheasants in Minnesota. We realized we needed to raise additional money and decided the best way to do that was starting chapters on a county-wide basis and let them keep the money and work with their farmer neighbors to do woody cover, nesting cover and food plots adjacent to key pheasant wintering areas. Nothing in that formula has had to change," Finden said.

The policy of allowing chapters (Minnesota's Kandiyohi County was PF's first chapter) to keep all funds they raised was crucial to PF's growth and local habitat success—and still is. PF's national office is funded by memberships, merchandise sales, corporate partners and various fundraisers.

But there was more to PF's early success.

"The Farm Bill, which we've been active on since day one, has really proven to be the savior for pheasants and other ground nesting birds. People never think of that, but when we started PF there weren't such things as private lands programs. All those programs have come about since PF was formed. We were the forerunners in the United States to work one-on-one with farmers to develop wildlife habitat. That was unique," said Finden, who still serves on PF's national board of directors.

Finden was never one to buy into the naysayers, in fact, he seems at his best when told something won't work. "People didn't think it was possible to do. They didn't believe farmers were good stewards of the land. Things were bad, but we found there were more farmers willing to work with us than we had money. It was obvious from PF's early days that there was a need and farmers were receptive."

Finden believes in keeping things simple. "It's pretty simple stuff when you think about it. It's not rocket science. "'Hey man,'" Finden role plays as is if he were talking to a farmer. " 'Do you want to plant a couple trees and leave a row of corn if we give you a couple hundred bucks.' It was absolutely the right thing to do for pheasants."

The problem for pheasants was also obvious to PF's co-founder—though some disagreed. "Habitat loss was the primary reason for pheasant decline. We hit that right on the head. People used to say, 'Oh, it's the pesticides, skunks and raccoons.' In fact, it was the government telling farmers they needed to farm fencerow to fencerow—and they did it. I remember hearing that and thought, 'Oh here we go,' and the pheasant declined with the habitat. Just in Minnesota alone during the 1960s and 70s we put 5 million new acres into production that was pasture, fencerows and poor land that never should have been farmed. Well, that's where the pheasants lived."

The millions of acres of habitat Pheasants Forever chapters have created, restored and improved nationwide will attest to the success of that simple, early philosophy.

Today's leadership

Finden, who was running Pheasants Forever from his basement in 1985, soon needed some accounting help to manage the growing organization. In 1985 PF had 12 chapters and 1,000 members, but that was changing fast and the organization needed to organize itself soon or risk faltering.

"An accounting friend, Dan Peterson called Finden and offered to help. Dan, a tax expert, soon realized PF needed a small business accountant not a tax expert. So Dan came down the hall and volunteered me to go out and meet with Finden. I was a hunter, Dan was a friend, so I did it," said Howard Vincent.

Vincent helped PF out for several years. By 1987, however, he realized PF's phenomenal growth required the organization hire a finance director. He suggested Finden post the job, which he did.

"Finden called me in April 1987 for breakfast, and asked me why I didn't apply for the job. I told him I didn't know it was posted. Jeff then handed me a pile of resumes and said either take the job myself or find someone else to do it. So, I started work in July figuring I'd stay a few years to help establish PF's accounting and administrative infrastructure and move on. My first year I hit the road for PF, doing 30 banquets as well as chapter starts and state meetings. There was something new and interesting every year. The upshot is—I got the bug and stayed."

Thirteen years later in 2000, Vincent was selected to replace the retiring Finden as PF's chief executive officer.

Vincent remembers the day to day challenges of those early days. "Leaving chapter dollars local created

A hen pheasant walks through the snow near Dickinson, North Dakota.

a lot of problems at first. We couldn't build our national structure as fast. Those first 8-10 years there were Thursdays we didn't have money for payroll," Vincent said.

"But something magical always happened," he recalled. "I'd sit with Jeff and tell him we couldn't make payroll. We'd agree not to take checks. But the next morning a check would come from somewhere and we'd make payroll. It was spooky. That formula kept us lean and mean in those days – a philosophy that continues up until today." Vincent said.

Another important factor that kept PF going in those early days was enthusiastic support from some well-known and even famous Minnesotans.

Early board members such a Vikings football coach Bud Grant; Norb Berg, deputy chairman of Control Data; Dave Vesall, Minnesota Department of Natural Resources; and Dennis Anderson gave PF the early credibility it needed. "People would see these high-profile leaders on our board and say, 'Oh, you're a serious organization,' " Vincent recalled. "We had incredibly talented, high visibility people. We needed that to attract new supporters."

More to come

Vincent's early experiences at PF began changing his mind about only serving a short stint. **"Soon I was falling in love with Pheasants Forever. I developed a belief in what was happening. It was no longer a job, but a calling. I was leaving something for my boys. Doing something for the environment, leaving a legacy for future generations. It had turned into a life mission."**

Vincent's longtime experience at PF helped him imagine a vision for the organization's future. "One of my goals is to give PF a larger profile in the national wildlife conservation community. PF has accomplished that by becoming a charter member in the American Wildlife Conservation Partners (a group of the nation's leading conservation organizations) and having a consistent presence at other professional wildlife conferences around the country. This gives PF a role in influencing national conservation policy, in debates that chart the future of conservation and our hunting heritage. It has given us a larger role on the national conservation stage." One result of PF reaching out nationally was the appointment of the organization to the North American Wetlands Conservation Council, U.S. Department of the Interior.

Vincent said that while PF is helping lead the nation's conservation movement and its broader agenda, it would remain loyal to its core mission—habitat and dedicated volunteers that do the work.

"PF can always do more and do it better. We understand our core mission is habitat and education, but at the same time we're looking for better and more efficient ways to achieve those goals. Keep your eyes on Pheasants Forever. There's much more to come."

(LEFT) Autumn harvest: a backlit Brittany points in good stubble.

(RIGHT) A pair of rooster pheasants and a pair of Hungarian partridge hang from a fence post at Dakota Hills Lodge, Oral, South Dakota.

Professional dog trainer Paul Knutson leans into a shot at a rooster in heavy cover.

Hunting Tips

"When hunting the wily wingneck, one must be wary, wary quiet."
—Elmer Fudd

Strategies

A person should look at their lifetime of hunting opportunities and recognize there are only so many opening days, which are often some of the best hunting. Therefore make sure your friends, relatives, spouse, or boss don't plan on your attendance on opening day. —*Joe Duggan*

Pheasant hunters new to an area need to do a little research. If you have any landowner or hunter contacts, use them. That will be a good starting point as you can base your first year's hunt in that area. Using downtime before or after the hunt to scout the countryside will pay handsome dividends in the future.—*Lee Harstad, South Dakota Department of Tourism and avid hunter*

(ABOVE) *Public land often gets hunted fairly hard. The trick is to find those out-of-the-way pockets that most hunters wouldn't even attempt to conquer. Whether it be six-foot-high cattails or a distant swath of CRP, that's where the birds will be.*—Lee Harstad, South Dakota Department of Tourism and avid hunter

(ABOVE) *Farmers are the best source of information when trying to find a good spot to hunt pheasants. They know where the birds are in their area. Talk to them before the season begins.*—Berdette Zastrow, Pheasants Forever National Board member and author Women's Guide to Hunting

Carry a red-tailed hawk call. When working running birds, hit the call. A rooster's instinct will be to freeze so the hawk doesn't spot him.—*Paul Hanson, Chairman, PF National Board of Directors*

Slow down. The pheasant is a great runner and that makes hunters feel that we need to go fast. Going too fast and rushing the dogs through cover causes us to go past tight-holding birds. If we slow down the birds that stick tight are the ones that will end up in the back of our bird vest.—*Craig Janssen*

(ABOVE) *Small parties—say two or three drivers and one or two blockers—risk being outflanked as wily ringnecks identify danger zones and run away from them. To prevent detection, blockers should kneel, crouch in ditches, or hide behind visual cover and be absolutely quiet and motionless until birds are heard or seen within range. Drivers should be aware of each blocker's hiding spot and keep all shots high against the sky.*—Ron Spomer

Reflushing roosters can net you an occasional bird you might not have got otherwise. The trick is to pursue only those birds that land in isolated patches of cover—small stands of cattails, clumps of sage surrounded by prairie, or grassy fencerows. Those that land in big expanses of cover will be much more difficult to move a second time.—*Dave Carty*

After pushing cover adjacent to a plowed field, have your dog work the bare ground on the way back. Many times roosters will leave cover to hide in furrows behind clumps of dirt or corn stalk root balls.—*Mark Herwig, Editor, Pheasants Forever Publications*

One or two hunters can surround pheasants in a big field through trickery. Stop at one end of the field and slam a door or talk as if getting ready to hunt. Then quietly but quickly drive to another side of the field and repeat. Hit one more side, then silently move to the final side to begin your quiet approach. Birds will be confused and more likely to hold. Similarly you can leave blaze orange caps or jackets on corner fence posts as blockers. Try a portable radio or two tuned to talk stations.—*Ron Spomer*

A lone hunter can drive a big CRP field by pushing its edges to its corners repeatedly, then cutting across its center to surprise birds that thought they were hiding. In a big field with many birds, one hunter can work like this for hours and never run out of birds.—*Ron Spomer*

When you have successfully worked pheasants into a corner or at the end of a pheasant drive, reload quickly after shooting because more often than not there will be multiple flushes.—*Dale C. Spartas*

Pheasants often develop patterns that can be used to your advantage. For example, if the birds flush from a certain cover on a day with a north wind, they probably will the next time, too. Out-smart them. —*Michael Pearce*

It's possible to predict pheasant flights to and from feed fields and set up under them. This is very useful in small, fragmented landscapes where birds are roosting and feeding on property you can't hunt. —*Ron Spomer*

Orange armies aren't the only way to succeed in big fields. One quiet hunter can do well behind a good dog left to follow its nose. Enter the field unseen and be as quiet as possible. If hunting with a buddy, have him quietly work ahead of the dog to cut-off running birds.—*Michael Pearce*

Hunting islands in rivers can produce a number of opportunities. It is best to drop off one or two shooters at the lower end of the island while hunters and dogs push down from the upper end.—*Dale C. Spartas*

Hunting in the snow can be quite productive for two reasons: It keeps other hunters from venturing out, and snow allows you to 'track' birds. Although it's unlikely you'll be able to follow an individual set of tracks to a rooster, numerous tracks let you know there are birds nearby, saving the time of hunting unproductive areas.—*Dave Carty*

(ABOVE) When hunting along rivers and creeks, post one member of your party along the banks. Roosters flushed from riparian habitat almost always fly over water.—Dave Carty

(ABOVE) Hunt late season birds. A little South Dakota weather can turn a good hunt into a great hunt. Birds bunch up tight in cold weather, allowing you to focus on heavy cover. It's also easier to gain access to private property as many resident hunters have put away their shotguns for the year.—Lee Harstad, South Dakota Department of Tourism and avid hunter

Pheasants are tough. If I hit a bird and he's falling with his head up (alive), I don't hesitate to pay the insurance with the left barrel.—*Craig Janssen*

Always keep your eye on a pheasant you think you missed. Pheasants can absorb a lot of shot. It's not unusual for them to tower or fly 200 yards or more and then simply drop from the sky.—*Larry Brown*

(ABOVE) No other snow is as good as the season's first snow. It catches young-of-the-year birds off-guard and confuses them. Look for any habitat with cover higher than a pheasant's head. They'll be seeking protection from hawks and will hold extremely well.—Michael Pearce

(BELOW) Whenever possible get around the front of a pointing dog that has pinned a bird. By pinching the bird between the hunter and the dog you will be more likely to get a close flush.—Dale C. Spartas

Shooting

Most hunters are over gunned and under shot. If you want to shoot well, shoot a lot.—*Dale C. Spartas*

Shoot clay targets before the season starts. Don't just take your gun out of the closet opening morning.—*Bill Benson, Iowa pheasant hunter and conservationist*

One well-timed shot is better than five quick ones.—*Michael Pearce*

Count one-thousand-one as you ride the lead on a rooster to make sure you're swinging smoothly and out in front of the bird.—*Michael Pearce*

(ABOVE) *Hunters with or without dogs should jump on fallen birds immediately. When you knock down a bird, lock your eye on the spot and race toward it, chamber empty, of course. Then stop and listen for rustling vegetation or beating wings. Hang your cap on a stalk to mark the spot and search out from there.—Ron Spomer*

From time to time a shot bird falls so close that you could reach out and catch it. Don't. More than one outfielding hunter has broken his hand or seen it pierced by a jagged wing bone.—*Ron Spomer*

When shooting a break-open gun, never throw empty shells in the field. Shotgun shells are not biodegradable. Leaving them in the field is littering and tells other hunters this a a good place to hunt.—*Dale C. Spartas*

Copper-plated premium shells in shot sizes 6, 5, or 4 are very effective on late-season pheasants.
—*Dale C. Spartas*

Dogs

The best pheasant-hunting dog is your buddy's dog.
—*Jeff Finden, PF co-founder, first CEO and National Board Member*

During late-season hunts I always carry an extra whistle in an inside pocket of my hunting coat. This comes in handy if my primary whistle freezes up.
—*Jerry Robinson of Okoboji, IA, an avid bird hunter and Life Member of Pheasants Forever*

(RIGHT) *The most important command for a flushing dog is for it to sit on the whistle. A dog that cannot be stopped will flush birds out of range, resulting in missed opportunities and frustrations.—Dale C. Spartas*

(ABOVE) *Hunters don't traditionally place bells or electric beeper collars on close-working Labs and springers, but they should if they want to keep track of the dogs in heavy cover. Even a slight breeze will camouflage a dog's motion and noise in tall cover, but a clanging bell or electronic tone usually carries well so you can face the action and avoid those frustrating flushes to your left when you thought the dog was on your right.—Ron Spomer*

(ABOVE) Love your hunting dogs, they are more than a hunting tool. They are family first.—Janet VanDerBeek, wife, great mother, and avid PF supporter

If possible when hunting a large field, use flushing dogs the first time through. Then go back through the field with pointing dogs. Pheasants that let you walk past them the first time will use the same strategy again, holding perfectly for a point.—*Dale C. Spartas*

In hot, dry habitat you must carry sufficient water for you and your dog. Save limited vest space by using a heavy-duty zip-lock bag for Rover's bowl. Hold it up as he drinks and he'll get it all without spilling a drop. This is more efficient than squirting water into his mouth.—*Ron Spomer*

It's best to not feed your dog before a hunt, lest he possibly develop twisted gut, but you can boost his lagging energy with a light mid-day snack of moist burger style dog food that comes in foil packs. —*Ron Spomer*

Reduce lost birds: hunt with a well-trained dog. Hunter interviews by the Iowa DNR show that parties with dogs lost only one bird in 10 downed, compared to two to three birds out of 10 for hunters without dogs.—*Larry Brown*

When bragging about one's dog, remember: when the tailgate drops, the bullshit stops.—*Dr. Bill Long*

Most pheasant hunters will let you insult them all the time, their wives most of the time, and their children occasionally. But never say anything bad about their hunting dogs! The proper comment would be, "He could be a pretty decent dog with a little more work." —*Michael Pearce*

Clothing and gear

Believe it or not, a simple change into fresh socks can add miles to your hunt. Tired, sore, wet feet wear you down. Thick, dry socks perk you up. Carry spares in your vehicle or vest and change when your dogs are barking. To reduce blisters and hot spots, change boots, too. The slight difference in fit makes a big difference over hours of walking.—*Ron Spomer*

I have found ankle-fit hip boots a standard part of my hunting gear. I often hunt the cattails and wetland areas for pheasants. With a pair of hip boots you don't have to stop when things get a little soggy or you come to a drainage ditch.—*Joe Duggan*

If your boots are leaking or wet, sandwich a plastic bag between a light and heavy pair of socks. Your feet will be warm and dry at the end of the day. —*Dale C. Spartas*

(ABOVE) Make sure your game bag is deep enough to carry three or four roosters or you may lose one or two. You do not want a bag that hangs down past your butt where it will bounce and slap with every step. The bag's bottom should fall low against the small of your back, but its sides should stand at least ten inches high.—Ron Spomer

To dry out wet boots, wad up newspaper and stuff it tightly into the boots. The newspaper acts like a sponge, drawing out moisture.—*Dale C. Spartas*

I keep a few old bath towels in my truck. They are useful in so many ways, from drying off wet dogs to washing hands after cleaning birds.—*Jerry Robinson of Okoboji, IA, an avid bird hunter and Life Member of Pheasants Forever*

The experience

Bring your kids. Hunting in South Dakota is a tradition and involving your children in the hunt is a great way to keep the tradition.—*Lee Harstad, South Dakota Department of Tourism and avid hunter*

One of the joys of pheasant hunting is remembering past hunts. I keep a journal in which I record the facts of each hunt. I also carry a small camera to visually record each hunt.—*Jerry Robinson of Okoboji, IA, an avid bird hunter and Life Member of Pheasants Forever*

Pheasant meat is too hard earned and flavorful to let it get freezer-burned by oxygen. Either vacuum seal your birds or freeze them in water.—*Michael Pearce*

The mark of a trophy bird is its spurs. Yearlings will have glorified pimples with rounded edges. Two-year-olds will have spurs about ⅜ inch with nice points. Anything ¾ inch or better is a trophy.—*Michael Pearce*

A bird with long, black, sharp spurs has survived at least one season, and his long tail will often add to his trophy status. But when many of these veterans show up in your bag, it's not good news. It's a sign that reproduction has been poor, and the total season harvest will almost certainly be below average.—*Larry Brown*

The key to our being able to harvest 75 roosters off of our 280 acre farm is to hunt our ground only one day each week. We only have 65 acres of habitat on our 280, so putting contour strips on the hills and buffer strips around the streams and pond helps to create as much edge as possible. To maximize pheasant habitat, plant tall native grasses, excellent year-round cover and especially protection from winter storms.
—*Kenny Snyder, avid pheasant hunter and PF chapter founder and active volunteer*

The best pheasant-hunting tip I can offer anybody is to **join Pheasants Forever.** Putting more habitat on the ground is the best way to improve your pheasant hunting.—*Howard Vincent, PF CEO*

(ABOVE) *Hunting rooster pheasants is a great way to have fun and build relationships. We started in 1981 with father and son groups. We've found that after a full day of hunting that teenagers are much easier to relate to.*—Cal Veurink, outfitter, Veurink's Dakota Outdoors

(RIGHT) *Many pheasants are crippled because they're hit low and in the rear, and the shot fails to reach any vital organs. Focus on the head and shoot high and in front for neatly taken birds.*—Larry Brown

Iowa Pheasants

Larry Brown

"Is this heaven?" asks Shoeless Joe Jackson as he emerges from the corn onto the baseball diamond in the movie "Field of Dreams."

"No," replies Kevin Costner's character. "It's Iowa."

To many pheasant hunters, Iowa is pretty close to heaven. It's been a top ringneck state for decades. During the 1990s, Iowa and South Dakota flip-flopped back and forth as numbers one and two in the nation in total season harvest. Outside of South Dakota, Iowa is the only state where hunters bag more than a million birds a year on a regular basis.

In several important respects, however, Iowa offers a very different hunting experience than South Dakota or the other popular pheasant states. For one thing, there are no true ranches in Iowa, nor are there very many really large farms. With the nation's most fertile soil, much of the land in Iowa is devoted to raising two row crops: corn and soybeans. Typical fields are 80 to 160 acres; a 320-acre field (half a square mile) is really big.

Fortunately for hunters, pheasants and agriculture coexist relatively well. Ringnecks fill the niche left behind by Iowa's native game birds—sharp-tailed grouse and prairie chickens—which could no longer survive once the pioneer farmers plowed up most of the native grass.

But pheasants also need grass and other heavier cover in which to nest and to shelter from harsh winters. Iowa's darkest days in modern times, in terms of pheasant habitat, came in the early 1980s when too much land was being cultivated and not enough set aside as wildlife habitat.

The Conservation Reserve Program (CRP), created as part of the 1985 federal farm bill, paid farmers to plant grass rather than row crops on highly erodible land.

CRP has remained part of the federal farm program ever since, and Iowa pheasants—and pheasant hunters—have benefited from it. Currently, the state has nearly 1.9 million total acres enrolled in CRP. Under the current farm bill, particular emphasis is being placed on CRP buffer strips—100-foot-wide strips of grass adjacent to waterways. In a highly successful, cooperative effort, the federal Natural Resources Conservation Service (NRCS), the Iowa Department of Natural Resources (DNR), and local Pheasants Forever chapters have worked together to encourage Iowa farmers to enroll in the buffer strip program. Result: Iowa leads the nation with 267,000 acres in buffer strips.

Those who haven't visited Iowa often imagine it as flat corn country, and that description is indeed accurate for some parts of the state. But there are significant differences in topography, and some parts of the state are much more intensively farmed than other parts. To thrive, pheasants need a combination of cover and food.

(*ABOVE*) *Don Borts and his pal, Cindy. Don, a retired Soil Conservation Service coordinator, has developed and enhanced his farm for wildlife, pheasants in particular. He realizes tremendous joy from allowing friends and family hunting privileges on his farm. Don is a staunch supporter of Pheasants Forever and an active member of the Keokuk County Chapter.*

(*LEFT*) *A pair of roosters flushes in the morning mist, Carole County, Iowa.*

(ABOVE) *"Hunter's Breakfast" at the Sigourney (Iowa) Fire Department. The place was buzzing with hunters and blaze orange. Over 250 breakfasts were served.*

(LEFT) *Ken Snyder, breeder of fine hunting Weimaraners, hunts through a feed plot/buffer zone in Carol County, Iowa. The habitat produced 20 flushes.*

They have that in most places in Iowa, but the mix will vary from region to region. Knowing a few more details about the state may help you decide which region you want to focus your hunting plans.

The DNR divides the state into thirds from north to south, and further slices those areas into thirds from west to east. This results in nine regions to examine.

The northwest, north central, and central regions are generally the flattest and most intensively farmed. They are also where the majority of the state's natural lakes and wetlands are located. (Iowa is on the southeast end of the "Prairie Pothole" region so familiar to waterfowl hunters.) After the harvest, pheasant cover will consist mainly of marshes, buffer strips along waterways, and road ditches. However, in spite of the lack of "big cover" such as large CRP fields, these regions typically provide some of the state's best hunting.

The west central region features more hills. The Loess Hills—a unique landform that rises above the Missouri River floodplain, almost all the way from Iowa's northern to southern borders—are a prominent geographic feature. This region does become less rolling as you head farther east. There is less row crop farming and more pasture and CRP ground than in the regions to its north or east. It usually has good bird numbers.

The three regions along the Missouri border contain the majority of the state's CRP land. Much of southern Iowa is rolling terrain, with more pasture and woods than any other region except the northeast. Crop fields are generally smaller than in the northern two-thirds of the state. Much of the terrain simply does not lend itself to intensive agriculture. A couple of decades ago, southern Iowa had some of the state's best bird hunting. It is still good in places, but bird numbers are generally down from past years.

East central Iowa is also mostly rolling terrain, but it's better for farming and is less forested than the southern regions. Traditionally, it is another of the state's very strong pheasant areas. The southern half of this region has quite a bit of CRP, but even farther north, there is a fair amount of "waste ground" that the birds find to their liking.

The northeast has Iowa's most rugged terrain and is the most heavily forested region. However, the western half of this region is good farming country, and like the north central region, often has good bird numbers. There are few large CRP fields, and bird cover will consist mostly of buffer strips and wetlands.

Compared to South Dakota, there is very little land leased for hunting in Iowa. It is also quite rare for Iowa landowners to ask hunters to pay a "trespass fee." After the harvest is over and the period of heaviest hunting pressure (first two weeks or so) has passed, it is fairly easy to get permission to hunt private land simply by knocking on a farmhouse door and asking politely. Small groups of two or three hunters will have better luck than large parties.

Often the most difficult part is determining who owns or farms the land, and then finding them at home.

County plat books (available at county courthouses) show clearly who lives where and owns what. They also show property boundaries. Farming practices have changed in recent years, and it is now typical for one farmer to own or lease ground in parcels scattered over several square miles. Farmers who give you permission for a particular piece of ground will often add that you might want to try "the Jones place," which may be three miles north, then a mile west, and then another mile north. With the help of a plat book, you can keep all that straight and have yourself more land on which to hunt.

Public Hunting and the Iowa DNR

Iowa has about 270,000 acres of land open to public hunting. Although that sounds like a lot, it is a small total in comparison to the Dakotas, Nebraska, and Kansas. Also, unlike those states, Iowa does not have a program that leases private land and makes it available for public hunting.

Most regions of the state do not have a lot of public hunting ground. There are, however, two exceptions. The first is the northwest region, especially around the "Great Lakes" region in Dickinson, Emmett, Palo Alto, and Clay counties. In those four counties, you will find more than 20,000 acres open to public hunting. Much of it is wetland/marsh habitat, although some is more traditional upland cover.

There are also large amounts of public land surrounding Iowa's four large reservoirs in the southern half of the state: Saylorville in Polk and Boone Counties; Red Rock in Marion County; Rathbun in Appanoose, Monroe, Lucas, and Wayne Counties; and Coralville (Hawkeye Wildlife Area) in Johnson County. Each of these areas is at least 10,000 acres in size, although a good share of that will be timber or more traditional waterfowl habitat.

You can get information on public land by checking the DNR website (www.iowadnr.com), where public areas are listed by county. In the case of many of the larger areas, there are also links to maps. Or you can call the DNR (515-281-5918) or write them at 502 E. 9th Street, Des Moines 50319-0034. They will send you free paper copies of "Public Hunting Areas of Iowa" and the current hunting regulations. Some public areas (mainly those managed for waterfowl) require the use of nontoxic shot

for pheasant hunting and will be listed in the regulations. But on most public areas, you may use lead shot.

Every August, the DNR conducts a "Roadside Survey." The results of this survey—usually available by mid-September—tell which regions have the highest bird numbers for that particular year.

Iowa's pheasant season dates and hunting hours have been the same for several years. The season opens the last Saturday in October and runs through January 10, which is also the expiration date of your hunting license. Shooting hours are 8 a.m. to 4:30 p.m. The bag limit is three roosters per day, up to a possession limit of 12.

The following regulations may differ from those found in other states:

To purchase a hunting license, anyone born after January 1, 1967, must have completed a hunter education course. Certificates issued by other states are acceptable.

There is no requirement to wear hunter orange, but it is recommended.

When transporting pheasants, a foot or fully feathered wing or head must remain attached to the body.

It is legal to hunt road ditches, but you cannot shoot within 200 yards of a building inhabited by people or domestic livestock, or a feedlot.

You need verbal permission to hunt on any private land. However, you may trespass (without a gun) onto private property without permission in order to retrieve dead or wounded game.

Jerry Robinson and Dick Lineweaver, life members and active volunteers of Pheasants Forever, stand by the entrance to a wildlife management area that is a cooperative effort between the Iowa DNR and P.F. These areas are paid for and managed by hunter dollars.

Kansas Pheasants

Michael Pearce

Ditch the fictitious associations with Dorothy and Oz. In reality Kansas is a place with a long heritage of bird hunting.

We have far more big-chested bird dogs than terriers named Toto.

Out here "gun control" means "four roosters with four shells."

Few prairie states offer as much diverse terrain as Kansas. Some places have cattail quagmires between small cropfields while others have fields of CRP or grain a mile or more in length!

All but the southeastern part of the state, basically east of highway 135, can hold pheasants. How many they hold depends on several things.

Winter-kill is seldom a deciding factor, at least not nearly as often as the condition of the wheat crop. A sizable majority of Kansas' pheasant nesting takes place in the wheat that's planted in the early fall and harvested in early summer. A lush crop makes for great nesting cover, while a drought bodes as poorly for pheasant hunters as farmers.

Ideally for hunters at least, there will be a wet spring where the wheat harvest is postponed for several weeks, giving chicks some time to hatch and become large enough to escape harvest machinery. Added moisture right after harvest helps, too, allowing sunflowers and other broadleafs to grow in the stubble, proving brood cover and insects needed for chick food.

As all over pheasantdom, changing farm practices haven't been kind to Kansas ringnecks. Strains of wheat are growing shorter and shorter, providing less cover. Where fields were once allowed to grow fallow after harvest they're often worked under or sprayed to kill weed growth.

Most years, populations changed mildly one way or the other, but extremes happen. In the mid-1990s we had a mild winter followed by an early spring, then a wet summer that hampered harvest and made it tough to work fields. Even in areas that had poor hunting the season before, things were good that fall. Some places went from fair to excellent!

On the other hand, the new century has come with three years of successive drought, each one taking major chunks from populations. Farms that produced 500 roosters five years earlier yielded only 30 in 2002...and that was the best hunting in the county.

Predict the weather a year or two in advance and you'll know the Kansas pheasant crop. Other than that, you weather the bad years and look forward to the better ones.

Regions

In terms of consistency over the last 30 years, northcentral Kansas probably beats other regions. It's not as prone to extreme drought as further west, and a rolling topography has left at least a few fields small enough to be hunted by a few guys and dogs.

The area is a pretty good mixture of cropfields, pastures, and CRP fields. Hard-core pheasant hunters generally concentrate on CRP fields near unworked grain stubble. There are still quite a few weedy draws where a couple of hunters can find pheasants mixed with decent (depending on the year) numbers of bobwhite quail. A good pheasant/quail day may be the best combo hunt in the nation, certainly up there with ruffed grouse and woodcock.

Northcentral Kansas has a fair amount of private lands enrolled in the Walk-In Hunting Area program and some decent public hunting areas...at least for the state that ranks 49th in the nation for the amount of public lands. Some of the northcentral public areas can have some great late fall and early winter mallard shooting on rivers and reservoirs. It all depends on the migrations, of course.

Northwest Kansas was once the prime region for pheasant hunting. Towns like Norton and Phillipsburg were as legendary on the southern prairies as Gregory and Winner further north. In the late 1990s, days of 200 or more flushes weren't uncommon amid the long CRP fields and big fields of milo and corn. But it was hit very hard by the drought that began about 2000. Some avid hunters have walked all day and seen only a handful of birds. But with a few good springs, the long-tailed birds could come back to this region of large land tracts. Public hunting areas in northwest Kansas are rare, but there are some nice tracts of walk-in hunting. Quail hunting can be fair some years and non-existent other years.

In the decades since Nixon was president, the flatlands of southwest Kansas have seem more habitat change than any part of the state. Thankfully CRP fields are very common because they're about the only cover left in this heavily farmed region. Some of the CRP fields are

The Kansas Grand Slam: a cock pheasant, a greater prairie chicken, and a bobwhite quail, all harvested while hunting with outfitter Don Zahourek of Glen Elder, Kansas.

downright huge, with a half-section or more of thick grasses. Most years this region has the most acres enrolled in the walk-in program.

The extreme corner of the state hosts the Cimarron National Grasslands and around 100,000 acres of public hunting. While it has some birds, it's better adapted for bobwhite and scaled quail hunting, which can range from good to terrible from year to year.

Drought can also take a heavy toll on pheasant recruitment in this region and after a truly miraculous turnaround in the mid- and late 1990s, the new century has gotten off to a bad start. Again, all it takes is two wet springs in a row and fortunes can change.

Southcentral Kansas seldom offers excellent pheasant hunting but it's seldom really poor, either. More heavily farmed than northcentral Kansas, it has a variety of habitats ranging from CRP fields to wetlands, evergreen shelterbelts and old homesteads. The area has a fair amount of public lands, including walk-in areas, but their closeness to Wichita and Hutchinson means a lot of hunting pressure.

Like northcentral Kansas, you never know what's going to flush when your dog points in this region. Mixed bag days with pheasant and quail are the norm rather than the exception. The region can hold a lot of ducks and geese in the right years.

A rooster flushes from a creek bottom in front of Jeff McPeak and Don Zahourek. Note that the bird is flying towards Don and Jeff has not raised his gun.

Only on rare occasions has northeast Kansas had pheasant hunting that compares with more noted parts of the state. Still, it's given some enjoyable hunts with quail mixed in. Generally the fields are smaller than in other parts of the state, and the land is more hilly with draws and creek bottoms mixed with CRP fields. Covers are usually small enough that just a couple of buddies can work them with decent dogs.

Walk-in areas aren't as common as further west, though there are some scattered public areas. Having communities like Kansas City, Lawrence, and Topeka in the region can make for heavy pressure on such areas.

Hunting Access

It's still possible to get access to private lands in Kansas, though not nearly as common as it was before non-resident deer hunting lead to increased leasing of properties. Generally the further away from population areas the better, and the smaller your hunting party, the better your odds. Forget about opening weekend or around holidays; most places are reserved for family or friends.

Your best contact could be a local sportsman. Try to make contact with a local Pheasants Forever chapter or with the small-town church of your home denomination. You'll help your cause mightily if you make contacts months before the season, and if you offer to trade a trip for a trip. I know of several lasting friendships that started with a traded fishing trip off the California coast for central Kansas quail and pheasant, and Michigan grouse and woodcock for southwest Kansas roosters.

Strong relationships can be made once you get your boots in the door of a good landowner. My advice to some inquiring Cajuns was to bring seafood as thank-you gifts. The first year they handed out gallon bags of fresh shrimp. The second year they started a complete seafood boil for local landowners. The third year they couldn't have hunted all the land open to them if they'd have stayed a month!

As stated, Kansas is poor for state-owned public land, with maybe two dozen reservoirs scattered about that have public spots nicely managed for wildlife. Some of them aren't too bad for those who will search out the distant nooks and crannies. Ditto for the few other public areas scattered about, including three or four wetland areas like Cheyenne Bottoms and the Jamestown Wildlife Area.

But the state has become downright rich with leased private lands within its Walk-In Hunting Area program. Other than the standard hunting license, sportsmen need no special permit to enjoy the program that's averaging almost one million acres a year!

Most of tracts are big CRP fields in western Kansas where bird numbers crashed severely near the turn of the current century. Still, when pheasant numbers were good some hunters had pretty good success.

Largely unheard of two decades ago, Kansas now holds scores of hunting guides and outfitters. Services range from daily trespass fees to five-star accommodations and totally guided trips. Take note that many are opting for "controlled shooting areas," which translates into released birds. Some put the birds out five minutes before the hunt and others occasionally add a few released birds to areas with wild pheasants to insure some action. A few years back, several outfitters were caught trying to

pass off released birds as pure wild birds. It's wise to check references and avoid guarantees.

For a listing of guides, try the state's two guide organizations at www.huntkansas.org or www.huntguide.com.

For all around pheasant hunting information, contact the Kansas Department of Wildlife and Parks, 512 SE 25th, Pratt, KS 6714 (620) 672-5911, www.kdwp.state.ks.us

Pheasant season opens the second Saturday of November and closes Jan. 31. Late-seasons success depends on the snow. The daily limit is four roosters, with 16 in possession on or after the fourth day. Quail season runs the same, except for the western one-third of the state where it opens the third Saturday of November (daily limit of eight, 32 after the fourth day). Prairie chicken season will be open for all or most of the pheasant season, depending on the area (daily limits of two or one, depending on the area, eight or four in possession after fourth day). Waterfowl seasons will be open for much of pheasant season. Check current regulations for specific zones and season dates.

Fall turkey season will be open throughout the season for much of central and eastern Kansas. Limits are as high as four per season. Dogs are legal during the fall seasons in Kansas. (My lab loves scattering and retrieving yearling poults!)

Guns don't need to be plugged or cased during transportation. Blaze orange is recommended but not mandatory. Shooting hours are from one-half hour before sunrise to sunset.

A Kansas Walk In Hunting Area. There are more than one million acres enrolled in this program and the areas are open to hunting with the purchase of a Kansas hunting license.

Minnesota Pheasants

Michael Furtman

I paused, panting, on the prairie. Despite cold fingers, numb where they gripped the old shotgun, my steamed eyeglasses and a wet spot between my shoulder blades revealed the heat of my exertion.

I had caught up to my black lab, Wigeon, where she'd disappeared into cattails bunched along the edge of a frozen pothole and marked her progress by the whipping tops of cattails scattering their downy seed pods. There was no hearing her over the sucking of my own breath. After the pause, I too stepped into the wall of cattails.

In that instant the prairie that had seemed so empty of all but the dog and me erupted into a confusion of life. A white-tailed deer burst from where it had been crouching to avoid the dog, so near to me that had I extended my shotgun I could have touched it. Snow, scattered from the cattails, hung momentarily in the air,

each crystal glittering in the lowering sun. Had I time, I'd have paused to admire it. But the chase was still on.

The dog traded directions, and as she did, pheasants flew from the far end of the marsh. A great wave of birds launched into the sky, every one of them out of shotgun range, the roosters snubbing me with their cackling laugh. Wigeon surged into an opening before me, her tongue lolling and red with exertion, her face clouded by snow and cattail down. I called her to my side and calmed her before we scoured the rest of the marsh. Of the pheasants, there was naught but their three-toed tracks and enough scent to drug the dog. Beaten, we walked wearily back toward the truck through the skiff of snow. On a rise, I turned to the slough and silently saluted the birds that had so handily eluded us.

From the knoll I scanned the horizon. The island of grass through which we had labored, so full of life, ended but a quarter mile away. Beyond, an ocean of black earth swept to the end of our sight, interrupted only by a few trees and some distant farm buildings. Roads diced the country into mile-sized squares—an immense

checkerboard. This well-ordered world we saw—well-ordered if you are a farmer—struck me then, as it always does, as a melancholy place, manipulated within an inch of its life.

Yet I love it here. Late in the year, when the sun never seems to rise much above half-mast, when thin gray clouds hinting of winter scud across the endless sky and cold winds hiss through the grass, I come to these grasslands to chase pheasants.

A creature of the North Woods, I am nonetheless drawn to prairie Minnesota by its remnant wildness. Each autumn I long to walk where the horizon is unbounded, to feel the tug of tall grass at my boots, to listen to the geese and cranes pass overhead, and to watch the never-ceasing quartering of a fine dog as it is dragged along by the intoxicating scent of a pheasant. I drive past the ubiquitous No Trespassing signs—including a huge, hand-painted one ("Don't Even Think of Hunting Here") that guards a barrens of dirt and stubble where, even if I had hunted, I would have had a hard time finding a field mouse. And when I pull up to a yellow Wildlife Management Area sign, or a green

one proclaiming Waterfowl Production Area, I feel a huge sense of welcome and a debt of thanks to those who created these public lands.

This testimony to change on a gargantuan scale is no indictment of farmers, who perform a vital task. But as I drive the miles of roads, see the fence-row-to-fence-row farms, tick off the seemingly endless miles of drainage ditches, I cannot help but wish we had been as farsighted in protecting prairie as we had been in reserving forests.

No greater champion of these prairies ever existed than Richard Dorer who—as state supervisor of game—dreamed of preserving prairie wetlands and uplands at a time when their destruction was rampant. Part preacher, part field general, Dorer talked in coffee shops and at meetings to all who would listen to his Save the Wetlands plan, his idea for a surcharge on small-game licenses to purchase some 200,000 acres of prairie lands and waters.

Despite his energy, the struggle must have been disheartening for this beefy man. With the post-World War II boom in full swing, he had to know he was working against an unrelenting headwind of contrary goals. Beginning in the late 1940s, as he wound his way across the state to preach, surely he saw yet more prairie plowed and watched draglines drain thousands of wetlands that vanished during the years it took for his dream to become law.

What sustains such dreams? Did he ever get angry as he drove the country roads trying to organize the state's then-unorganized hunters? If the prairie is a miracle of creation, so too is the will of a person so bent on its preservation that he can snatch thousands of acres away from the plow.

"Conservation is the militant defense of natural resources," Dorer wrote. The use of "militant" might today brand him as some kind of extremist. And in the 1950s, saving wetlands and grass might have labeled him as an oddball. But it took the organization of a military campaign to create his program, and though it then may have seemed odd, today it is clear that his plan to save prairie and wetlands was truly farsighted.

From Dorer's time on, Minnesotan's have been active—even passionate—about protecting, improving and acquiring pheasant habitat in the state's primary

A rooster flushes from heavy cover in southern Minnesota. The shadow of the hunter bearing down on the pheasant is below and slightly to the right of the bird.

pheasant range. One such endeavor of which most readers will be familiar is the grand conservation group, Pheasants Forever. This organization, now twenty years old, began in Minnesota and was conceived by Dennis Anderson, then a young outdoor writer for the St. Paul Pioneer newspaper.

Having gone to college in Morris, Minnesota, a place right on the northern edge of the state's best pheasant range, Anderson became an avid rooster warrior. But as the years passed, and pheasant hunting continued to decline because of poor land use practices, Anderson used his bully pulpit in the newspaper—and a lot of hard work behind the scenes—to fund and incorporate this, one of the very best, habitat conservation organizations.

Because of efforts of Pheasants Forever, Ducks Unlimited, the Minnesota Waterfowl Association, the Minnesota Department of Natural Resources and the U.S. Fish and Wildlife Service, tens of thousands of acres of wetland and upland habitat have been acquired over the years. In Minnesota, wetlands are as important to pheasants as they are to ducks, for the harsh winters—always a key limiting factor in pheasant populations here—demand dense cover. In many cases, wetlands, with their cattails and other marsh plants, provide the *only* winter cover in prairie Minnesota. Thus the partnership of waterfowl and pheasants groups provides multiple benefits to wildlife and hunters.

Pheasants are a bird of southern Minnesota. If you drew an east-west line across the middle of the state, you'd largely define the regions where pheasants are and are not found. To the south, there are pheasants. To the north—which is mostly forest land—there are virtually none.

Hunter and conservationist Les Johnson, standing in a CRP field at sunset, takes a moment to admire and reflect on the natural beauty of the land. We moved more than 50 birds when we hunted Les' farm. Les said that 10 years ago, before the property was enrolled in CRP and managed for wildlife, we would have been lucky to see one or two pheasants.

But that doesn't mean that all of southern Minnesota is good pheasant range. The best is generally found in west central and southwest Minnesota. Year to year the best areas change based on snowfall amounts, but it would be a safe bet that if you planned your hunt in the part of Minnesota adjacent to the South Dakota or Iowa borders, you'd be in the prime pheasant range.

That said, not all of this is even equal. Access to hunting land is as important to hunters as are bird populations, and the fact is that in the far south of the state, public lands are not as abundant as most hunters would like. That is slowly changing, as the DNR and its partners work to acquire land, but for now, the highest percentage of public lands are in the west-central part of the state.

There are 1,300 state-owned Wildlife Management Areas in Minnesota, providing 1.1 million acres of habitat. Although not all of these are in pheasant range, the majority are. These state lands—the result of Dorer's vision—and the additional approximately 100,000 acres of federal Waterfowl Production Areas, provide the bulk of public pheasant hunting opportunities in this state. While it is possible to get access to private land if you are persistent enough, the fact is that many of the farms in pheasant range are so intensively farmed that there is little hunting to be had, even if you could gain access.

In my experience, two strange dichotomies are that pheasant hunting can often be better on the fringe of the "prime" pheasant range, or during years when pheasant numbers are somewhat diminished. The reasons are the same in both cases—fewer hunters, meaning more birds per hunter, even though the number of roosters is lower. In years when the DNR predicts good pheasant hunting, folks who otherwise would not pursue the birds break out their dusty shotguns and the public lands are pounded hard. But if predictions are less than rosy, then only the dedicated venture forth. The same can be true on the fringe of the best pheasant range—fewer birds, but fewer hunters.

Late season pheasant hunting is also a great way to escape the crowds. Minnesota's pheasant season generally opens in mid-October. During many years, crops are still standing, so hunting is tough. Most crops, though, will be down by early November, and the combination of the opening of deer season and the advent of much colder weather (and snow) means fewer hunters. Either they are pursuing whitetails or they simply don't like the cold. But for those with a tough dog and stout legs, hunting Minnesota roosters, even into December, can provide some high quality pheasant hunts. Yes, there are fewer birds by this time, and those that remain now have PhDs in "escape-ology," but there is no denying the satisfaction of routing an old rooster out of snow-caked cattails.

Typically Minnesota's bag limit is two cocks per day. In a good year, hunters will kill about 350,000 birds. Not a huge amount compared to South Dakota, but when you consider that only a third of Minnesota is really prime pheasant country, that's not a bad harvest.

Western Minnesota is a glorious place, at least when one is following a fine dog through the big bluestem, or busting cacklers out of cattails. I know that as long as these legs will carry me, and I own a dog whose heart is as big as its legs are tough, you will find me here in November.

Contacts:

Minnesota Department of Natural Resources
500 Lafayette Road
St. Paul, MN 55155-4040
Telephone: (651) 296-6157 or (888) MINNDNR
http://www.dnr.state.mn.us/index.html

The DNR typically issues its pheasant forecast in early September after completing the August roadside counts. Results can be found on their website. In addition, maps of nearly every state Wildlife Management Area can also be found on line. Minnesota requires the purchase of a pheasant stamp. Non-toxic shot must be used in Wildlife Management Areas.

U.S. Fish and Wildlife Service

You may not think of the USFWS as a producer of pheasants, but indeed it is. About 100,000 acres of prime pheasant hunting in Minnesota are found on federal Waterfowl Production Areas administered by USFWS wetland districts. Maps and information on these WPAs are best obtained by wetland district—either contacting them directly or visiting their websites. Federal WPAs are closed to motorized traffic, but walking hunters are welcomed. Non-toxic shot is required. The districts in the best of Minnesota's pheasant range are listed below.

Litchfield Wetland Management District
(WPA: 146 units, totaling 32,828 acres)
971 East Frontage Road
Litchfield, MN 55355
Phone: 320/693 2849
Fax: 320/693 2326
http://midwest.fws.gov

Morris Wetland Management District
(WPA: 244 units, totaling 50,179 acres)
Route 1, Box 877
Morris, MN 56267 Phone: 320/589 1001
Fax: 320/589 2624
http://midwest.fws.gov

Windom Wetland Management District
(WPA: 59 units, totaling 11,445 acres)
Route 1, Box 273A
Windom, MN 56101-9663
Phone: 507/831 2220
Fax: 507/831 5524
http://midwest.fws.gov

The Peterson State Wildlife Management Area, a cooperative project between the Nobles County Chapter of Pheasants Forever and the Minnesota DNR, is a 640-acre wetland.

Nebraska Pheasants

David Draper

Field Editor, *Cabela's Outfitter Journal*

Autumn in Nebraska means two things—pheasant hunting and Cornhusker football. It's not unusual (in fact, I'd call it common) to see the two seemingly different pastimes come together every Saturday from the October pheasant opener until the bowl game on New Year's Day. Hunters clad in oilskin and orange gather around an open truck door parked alongside an expansive stubble field or crowd the small TV perched above every bar in diners across the state to cheer on their beloved Big Red.

Like football, some pheasant seasons in Nebraska are better than others, but winning seasons and full game bags are more-often-than-not the rule in the Cornhusker State. Nebraska annually ranks in the top five in number of birds harvested per hunter, with nearly half of those birds taken from the October opener until late November. Of course, this is also when the most hunters are afield. December sees about 35 percent of the total number of birds killed, while January makes up the final 15 percent.

There are more than 800,000 acres of federal and state lands open to hunting Nebraska and millions more private land that's just a knock and friendly smile away. Landowner permission is required to hunt on private land, whether it's posted or not. Much of Nebraska is ideal pheasant habitat, be it crop lands, CRP fields, brush-choked waterways, vast fields of native grasses, or a mixture of some or all of the above.

As a partner with Pheasants Forever, Nebraska's operates a walk-in program that opens up more than 135,000 privately held CRP areas to public hunting. The Conservation Reserve Program-Management Access Program (CRP-MAP) has proved to be a success among hunters and landowners alike. Maps available from the Nebraska Game and Parks Commission detail the location of each CRP-MAP area and list the type of wildlife you're likely to find there.

Southeast

Bordered on the north by the ubiquitous Platte River, on the east by the Missouri River Valley, veined with numerous other waterways, and dotted with lakes, the southeast part of Nebraska is a hunter's dream come true. Farm size increases as you travel across the region, from smaller acreages encircled by hedgerows in the extreme southeast to irrigated croplands in the west. There's also plenty of public land open to hunters and the chance at adding everything from quail to prairie grouse to hedgerow chicken, a.k.a. cottontails, to the game bag. The bad news? The region is also home to Nebraska's largest population base, so some public lands can take a real beating, especially during the opener and for a few weeks after. Later in the season, hunters have a greater chance of finding some quiet time afield.

There's more good news, though. The southeast also lays claim to tens of thousands of acres of CRP-MAP lands, as well as the highest number public areas in the state, with the most popular lying within the Rainwater Basin. This area, roughly from Kearney to York, primarily south of Interstate 80, is a network of Wildlife Management Areas (WMA) and Waterfowl Production Areas (WPA) that are managed to provide quality hunting opportunities. Expect reed-lined lakes, marshes, and tall-grass prairies—all of which are prime pheasant (and other wildlife) habitat. Other popular public areas include: Branched Oak Lake and Rockford Lake State Recreation Areas (SRA); Jack Sinn Memorial, Schilling and Pawnee Prairie WMAs; Hannon WPA; Elwood Reservoir and Harlan County Federal Reservoir.

Northeast

Maybe it's the proximity to the South Dakota or the friendly landowners or the acres and acres of CRP-MAP lands. Whatever the reason, the northeast corner of Nebraska is about as good as it gets when it comes to hunting the ringneck pheasant in the Cornhusker State. Rolling hills and river bottoms make up the bulk of the land in this corner of the country and it's all prime habitat. It's no wonder that this region typically leads the state in number of birds harvested.

You'll see a few hunters in the field, but there are enough opportunities up here for everyone, it seems. A knock on a door and a respectful inquiry will generally secure you more land than you can hunt in a weekend and, if you're lucky, an invitation to come back next year. Wayne, Cedar, Madison, and Antelope Counties are good places for the traveling hunter to use as a base for his or her excursions, with the city of Wayne being a traditional pheasant-hunter hot spot.

There are plenty of public hunting areas in the northeast, although many of them tend to be smaller in size. Don't discount them. They can offer fantastic wingshooting for pheasants, as well as a chance at quail and/or waterfowl. Some of the larger public lands include: Bazile Creek, Grove Lake, Yellowbanks, Prairie Wolf, and Wilkinson WMAs; Lewis and Clark Lake and Willow Creek SRA.

The Sandhills

With more than 20,000 square miles of grass-covered dunes, the Nebraska Sandhills, in the north-central part of the state, is one of the largest natural grasslands in the world. For wingshooters, the prairie chicken and sharptail grouse reign supreme among the rolling mixed-grass prairie. But pheasant abound as well, if you know where to look for them.

The country is dominated by sprawling ranches, but row-crop farming does exist and it's here and among the shelterbelt-lined homesteads where pheasant hunters should target the ringneck. The Ogallala Aquifer lies nearer to the surface here than anywhere else on the Great Plains, resulting in thousands of ponds, marshes, and lakes throughout the region. These reed-lined bodies of water are often thick with pheasants, particularly late in the season when frozen ground allows hunter access. Because population is sparse and the ranches are so huge, just one friendly handshake can gain a hunter access to thousands upon thousands of acres of land upon which he may not see another human.

As hard as it may be to do, ignore the 300,000 acres of public land tied up in the two national forests (McKelvie and Nebraska NF) and national wildlife refuge (Valentine NWR) open to hunting in the Sandhills. Not that there's not great hunting here. There

A hunter admires a sundown rooster near Nebraska's sand hills, where mixed bags of prairie chickens, sharp-tailed grouse, and pheasants are possible.

is. It's just that sharptails and prairie chickens dominate and pheasant hunters will have to work a little harder to roust up a cock bird. But don't let that deter you from visiting this region. In fact, done right, hunters can easily get a mixed game bag with just a short drive and interrupted by a few long walks. Cottonwood Steverson, Davis Creek, Milburn Diversion Dam, and Arcadia Diversion Dam WMAs and Calamus, Sherman, and Merritt Reservoirs are the largest pheasant-friendly public areas in the region.

The Southwest

If Nebraska has anything similar to opening day in Mitchell, South Dakota, it's here in the southwest. The occasion is celebrated here with night-before smokers and early-morning hunter's breakfasts. Drive down the main streets of McCook or Imperial on opening weekend and you're apt to see license plates from Colorado, Kansas, Missouri, and states far beyond, each attached to trucks filled with men, women, and children in orange and dog boxes with pointers and flushers alike. Here, pheasant is king.

An excellent place to find birds: corn fields provide food and shelter for upland birds, particularly pheasants.

This is big country. Rugged plains dotted with pivot-irrigated corn, alfalfa, and wheat. Two river systems course through the country and numerous creeks scar the landscape. Several irrigation reservoirs feed thirsty crops and provide acres of prime pheasant country open to the public. Opening-day armadas do well walking shoulder to shoulder across big fields, but the solitary hunter and a good dog has just as good a chance at filling his game bag by targeting shelterbelts, drainages, and the weed-choked corners of center-pivot fields.

Most of the good public land in the southwest is adjacent to the large irrigation reservoirs. The largest include Lake McConaughy; Sutherland, Enders, Red Willow and Swanson Reservoirs; Medicine Creek SRA and Clear Creek and Cedar Valley WMAs. And make sure to include a stop at Ole's in Paxton for a burger and a beer. Trust me, you'll be glad you did.

The Panhandle

This is the High Plains proper, with mile after mile of seemingly flat land covered from road ditch to road ditch with wheat, corn, and millet and cut nearly in half by the wide, fertile, North Platte river valley. Oh, and don't forget the scenic Pine Ridge escarpment just a few miles from the South Dakota border. Like the name suggests, the rugged ridge is dotted with pine trees and home to turkey, white-tailed and mule deer, elk, antelope, and even bighorn sheep.

Don't think this big country isn't bird country because pheasants abound and the region offers some of the best waterfowling in the world. If you're looking for a combo upland and waterfowl hunt, plan your visit to the Panhandle in late December and get ready for world-class wingshooting.

The Panhandle competes with the Sandhills for most acres of public land. The Pine Ridge offers a few hundred-thousand acres, much of it tied up in the Oglala National Grassland where prairie chickens and sharptails compete with pheasants for the bird hunter's attention. While much of the land bordering the North Platte River is tied up in leases, hunters can find good pheasant hunting access on private land just a few miles off the river. Conservation-minded farmers have also enrolled thousands of acres in the CRP-MAP program, making some great private land accessible to the pheasant hunter. The region also has a number of public areas, large and small that offer excellent hunting opportunities. Box Butte State Recreation Area, Oliver Reservoir, and the vast Crescent Lake National Wildlife Refuge are some of the top picks for pheasants.

General Regulations

The Nebraska Game and Parks Commission allows hunters three birds per day, with 12 in possession. Pheasant season traditionally runs from the last Saturday in October until January 31.

All Nebraska residents 16 years and older who hunt for game birds or game animals need a small game permit. All nonresidents, regardless of age, must obtain a permit. Small game licenses are valid January 1 through December 31. In addition, resident and nonresident hunters are required to have an annual Habitat Stamp to hunt game species. The Habitat Stamp is valid for the calendar year as dated. Licenses and stamps must be signed in order to be valid.

Any person 12 years of age or older, born on or after January 1, 1977, must have successfully completed a state-certified Hunter Education course prior to hunting and must have their valid Hunter Education card in their possession when hunting. Hunters under the age of 12 must be accompanied by a licensed hunter who is at least 19 years of age.

For a complete listing of Nebraska hunting regulations and guide to public hunting lands, contact the NGPC at P.O. Box 30370, Lincoln, NE 68503, by phone at (402) 471-0641 or via the Internet at www.ngpc.state.ne.us.

(TOP) *Hunting a vast CRP field. Upland birds, waterfowl, and numerous other types of wildlife benefit greatly from the more than 36 million acres of land enrolled in the Conservation Reserve Program.*

(ABOVE) *A cock pheasant looks up from feeding.*

(LEFT) *A very long-tailed rooster fills out a game bag for a hunter in tall reeds and cattails.*

North Dakota Pheasant Hunting

Dan Nelson

Pheasant hunting's best-kept secret is out of the bag. Pass the word: North Dakota has birds, and lots of them.

The pheasant boom of the 1990s attracted a stampede of hunters to high-profile ringneck destinations like South Dakota, Iowa and Nebraska, but only a few strays wandered into North Dakota. Of the 47,000 upland bird licenses sold there in 1990, out-of-staters grabbed fewer than 4,300.

The number of visiting hunters ticked steadily upward during the 1990s, reaching 14,000 in Y2K, and that's when it happened. The state's tourism slogan was "Discover North Dakota," and in 2001 non-resident pheasant hunters did: More than 22,000 of them flocked to the state that fall, a 60 percent increase over the previous year.

The ringneck harvest rose in lockstep. In 2001 resident and non-resident hunters combined to kill more than 421,000 roosters, the highest take since the soilbank program expired in 1963.

Unfortunately North Dakota's "discovery" as a pheasant destination hasn't come without a price. Pay-as-you-go-hunting, which was rare a decade earlier, has become increasingly common across the pheasant-rich southwestern corner of the state. In North Dakota land that isn't posted is open to hunting, but today many landowners host as many parties as they can reasonably handle. Accommodations in small-town motels must be secured months in advance.

The good news is that the North Dakota Game and Fish Department has developed an extremely successful Private Land Initiative (PLI) to complement hundreds of thousands of acres of state and federal land already open to public access. PLI Coordinator John Schulz says the Private Lands Open to Sportsmen (PLOTS) program had grown to 300,000 acres by 2003, nearly doubling in size since 2001.

The various private lands programs provide cost-sharing assistance for landowners wishing to develop and protect wildlife habitat. Programs under the PLI umbrella include habitat plots, food plots, forests, watersheds, wetlands, and waterbanks. In exchange for financial assistance, landowners provide free public access on enrolled acres.

Another innovative PLI project known as Conservation CoverLocks was developed by former information specialist Ted Upgren. CoverLocks provide 20-acre habitat-development sites within a quarter section (160 acres) of land. CoverLocks acres are protected by 30-year easements and the entire 160 acres are open to public hunting during that period.

But even at 300,000 acres, PLOTS represents a small portion of the public land open to hunting. Most of the state's 200,000 acres of Wildlife Management Areas (WMA's) are open to public access as are lands held by the Department of Agriculture, the state Forest Service, and the North Dakota State Land Department.

There also are thousands of acres of federal land open to hunting, including many US Fish and Wildlife Service Waterfowl Production Areas (WPA's) and National Wildlife Refuges, and land held by the US Forest Service, the Bureau of Reclamation, the Bureau of Land Management, and the US Army Corps of Engineers.

All of the state and federal lands open to the public are identified in color-coded maps contained in the Game and Fish Department's PLOTS Guide. The guide can be ordered by calling 701-328-6300 or by writing to North Dakota Game and Fish Department, 100 Bismarck Expressway, Bismarck, ND, 58502.

While the private-lands habitat work being conducted by Game and Fish is expected to yield huge wildlife benefits down the road, it's not the main reason North Dakota is flush with pheasants. Credit for healthy ringneck populations goes to Congress and Mother Nature.

When Congress authorized the Conservation Reserve Program (CRP) as part of the 1985 farm bill it paved the way for close to three million acres of North Dakota cropland to be converted to large blocks of grassy nesting cover. Pheasants thrive in CRP, and the pheasant numbers responded quickly.

Mother Nature did her part, too. Pheasants are imports that did not evolve with severe winter weather. Blizzards and extended periods of extreme cold take their toll. Fortunately, with a couple of notable exceptions North Dakota winters have been relatively mild during the last decade.

Historically the best hunting is found south of Interstate 29 and west of the Missouri River around towns like Mott, Elgin, Carson, Flasher, and Hettinger. Lowell Tripp, the state's long-time upland biologist, says most of the pheasant harvest still occurs in the southwest corner of the state, but is quick to add that the hunting is just as good in other, less publicized, areas of the state.

He says the central and south-central portions of North Dakota not only have excellent pheasant populations, they

In classic cover for sharptail grouse and pheasants, a tightly holding cock bird flushes in front of a hunter and a Brittany.

North Dakota has experienced tremendous gains in pheasant populations with the advent of CRP, as depicted by this field of pheasants in barley stubble adjacent to a CPR field.

also receive less hunting pressure. Counties cited by Tripp for quality hunting are Morton, Oliver, Mercer, McLean, Burleigh, and Emmons. Those counties all border the Missouri River system and have large blocks of Corps of Engineers land that's open to hunting.

Tripp says pheasant hunting is also good in the southeastern part of the state. The northwest corner of the state experiences population swings based mostly on winter weather. Only the northeast corner of the state, where winters can be brutal and nesting cover is sparse, lacks quality pheasant hunting.

Pheasant futures still rise and fall with weather, and one bad winter can knock ringneck numbers for a loop. That happened in the winters of 1991-92 and 1996-97, but thanks to CRP bird numbers rebounded quickly.

Across much of North Dakota's pheasant range the birds roost in dense CRP grass and, come morning, can be seen flying or walking to corn, wheat, sunflowers, or whatever food source is readily available. During the middle of the day birds often loaf in tree rows, fence lines, creek bottoms, or whatever cover exists adjacent to food plots. They'll feed again in late afternoon before returning to the CRP, often picking gravel along the way.

The pheasant season typically opens the middle of October, but in recent years politicians have discussed an early opener. North Dakota-bound hunters should check with the ND Game and Fish Department to learn the exact opening date. The season usually runs through the first week of January. The daily limit is three birds and the possession limit is 12. Legal shooting times are one-half hour before sunrise until sunset.

An upland bird license is good for the entire season and in recent years has cost $85. Hunters born after 1961 are required to have completed a hunter safety education course before applying for a North Dakota hunting license.

Other upland species available include sharp-tailed grouse and Hungarian partridge. Grouse numbers have been fairly strong across the western half of the state, and it's not uncommon for hunters to go home with a few bonus "sharpies." Partridge numbers took a hit from blizzards in 1991-92 and 1996-97 but have been slowly rebounding. The season on grouse and partridge opens in the middle of September. The state also has a mourning dove season, but typically most doves have migrated out of the state by the time pheasant season opens.

North Dakota also has some excellent waterfowl hunting. The state legislature recently placed a restriction on the number of non-resident waterfowl permits, so hunters planning to hunt both upland and waterfowl should apply early. Waterfowl licenses are good for 14 consecutive days or two seven-day periods and hunters are restricted to certain zones. Check the Game and Fish web site for details.

North Dakota's weather is predictably unpredictable, and hunters should be prepared for every possibility. The Halloween Blizzard of 1991 brought several feet of snow and wind chills around 50-below zero; the following year the temperature on Halloween was pushing 90. Indian summer can be replaced by a winter storm in a matter of hours, so hunters should pack accordingly.

A controversial law requiring non-resident hunters to obtain state-issued health certification for hunting dogs has been rescinded, but hunters are required to carry verification of rabies vaccinations for all dogs.

Hunters willing to pay a daily per-gun fee will have no trouble finding quality places to chase pheasants. Self-guided hunters will probably want to start on the public land and devote a portion of each day to visiting with landowners. Land enrolled in CRP is not automatically open to public access. Permission to hunt must be obtained on all posted land and is recommended even on land that's not posted.

Good sources of information include the Game and Fish Department, small-town chambers of commerce, and the state's Tourism Division. North Dakota Tourism publishes two guides that list some of the commercial outfitters along with motels, campgrounds, and small-town chambers of commerce. One is the Travel Guide and the other is the Hunting and Fishing Guide. To obtain those guides or to get additional information on hunting opportunities, call 1-800-HELLO-ND.

Licensing information and the PLOTS Guide can be ordered on-line at www.state.nd.us/gnf// or by calling the Game and Fish Department at 701-328-6300. The Game and Fish web site lists several maps that can be purchased through other state agencies.

South Dakota Pheasant Hunting

Lee Harstad

Did Meriwether Lewis and William Clark kick up any pheasants when they trekked through South Dakota some 200 years ago? Probably not—but if any modern-day explorers make tracks around South Dakota, it's a sure bet that they will run into pheasants somewhere along their path.

Pheasants and South Dakota. The names make a strong pair and are an even stronger draw for thousands of hunters every year. Some 150,000 hunters take to the field each year, and each hunter's bag averages around nine pheasants. In most years, the statewide ringneck population numbers close to six million.

Despite those outstanding figures, Chinese ring-necked pheasants weren't always the main target for South Dakota's hunters. South Dakota's first pheasant season took place in Spink County in 1919. Redfield,

the county seat and current home to some 3,000 residents, continues to draw hunters each season. Seasons took place in various parts of South Dakota until 1941, which marked the first statewide season. The pheasant has since become a staple piece on South Dakota's landscape, much like Mount Rushmore National Memorial, and it is the official state bird.

Habitat

So why have pheasants continued to flourish in South Dakota? One word can answer that: habitat. It may sound redundant by now, but habitat is the key to a successful pheasant population, and, in return, a successful pheasant hunting experience. The South Dakota Game, Fish and Parks Department knows the value of habitat and invests much time and money to continue the long-standing tradition of pheasants and hunting.

Pheasant management is actually quite simple: develop secure places for pheasants to reproduce, feed, and escape their enemies and you will have strong

A classic pheasant drive near Aberdeen, South Dakota. South Dakota hosts 150,000 pheasant hunters and has a statewide population of six million pheasants!

populations. The more habitat you create, the more pheasants you will have. Pheasant population numbers fluctuate annually with varying weather conditions, such as droughts, but the long-term levels of pheasant populations will be determined by°you guessed it, habitat. Find decent habitat in South Dakota, and pheasants won't be far behind.

Licenses

The necessary license is a South Dakota Small Game license. A nonresident small game license will get you 10 days of hunting. You can either take all 10 days in one chunk, or break it down into two five-day periods. That way, you can hit the early season birds and come back later in the year. One bit of advice, when filling out the license, put down the final week of the year for your second hunting dates. That way you can come back anytime during the season and dates can be changed. A small game license also entitles you to other upland birds like grouse, prairie chickens, and partridge. It varies each year, but many of the seasons overlap, allowing you to target a variety of birds on the same outing. And in many areas, it's not uncommon for a game bag to be filled with pheasants, grouse, and prairie chickens. Small game licenses are unlimited in South Dakota and hunters can purchase as many small game licenses as they like during the season.

Hunting opportunities

South Dakota has a plethora of public hunting availability, such as federal and state waterfowl and game production areas, and the successful Walk-In Area program. That Walk-In Area program opens up hundreds of thousands of acres of public hunting to sportsmen and women. For the past decade, GF&P has been working hard to maintain hunting heritage by providing hunting access on privately owned lands.

Tumbleweed Lodge provides elegant accommodations, great dinning, and fabulous hunting on 7,000 acres of superb pheasant habitat.

Bill Smith, GF&P biologist and Walk-In Area administrator, says the department does this through its local conservation officers contracting with landowners who have CRP or other valuable wildlife habitat.†"The landowner opens the land to unlimited, free public hunting, which is open to foot-traffic only hunting, in exchange for a small payment and other non-monetary considerations. It has been a great program and currently has more than 900,000 acres enrolled."††

GF&P publishes a Public Hunting Area Guide annually to assist hunters in finding a place to hunt. It is a free publication and includes all public hunting areas, including Walk-In Areas.

There are also a number of private hunting operations. Many of these operations dedicate their entire land tracts to pheasant hunting. Managing large blocks of land for wildlife is time-consuming and costly. To offset that cost as well as the cost of not producing crops, these operations apply a charge. These fees vary, but it's a guaranteed way to see a plentiful amount of birds. And these birds are wild. There are some operations that maintain or supplement bird populations by stocking pen-raised birds, but if the operation has proper cover, nesting habitat, and food, these practices are unnecessary. In fact, research shows that pen-reared birds have a success rate in the wild of 10 percent or less.

Where to hunt

The famous pheasant "triangle" in South Dakota extends from the Winner area in the southwest to the Mitchell area in the northeast and the Vivian-Kennebec area to the east. That being said, this area is hunted

fairly hard during the season. Public lands available to hunt in this area are more difficult to find, but it's still possible. A good plan in this area is to hire a guide or stay in one of the many lodges in the area. It's a surefire way to come across cloud after cloud of pheasants like the "good-old days."

Besides that "triangle," pheasants can be found just about anywhere you can find good habitat. The unofficial pheasant belt of South Dakota consists of an area east of the Missouri River to the South Dakota-Minnesota border. Pheasants are more plentiful in some areas than others, with pockets of birds to be found, but it's a good bet a day's hunt will provide some prime gunning action. Areas west of the Missouri River and along its banks can also be good, and a day's bag from that area can also include grouse and prairie chickens.

Glacial lakes and prairies

To narrow it down further, the James River Valley—stretching from the Sand Lake National Wildlife Refuge area until it spills into the Missouri River—has been a pheasant haven for both birds and hunters. The area is hunted fairly hard, but pheasant counts in these areas rank among the highest in the state. The most abundant public land tracts are located in the north-central portion.

Communities such as Aberdeen, Redfield, Huron, Watertown and others in this area are true wingshooting destinations. Despite the heavy traffic of hunters in these areas, birds can, and usually are, found.

But an unknown area can be just as successful with the right amount of research. Where there are birds there will also be hunters, but many times areas are overlooked. Areas in the northeast tip of South Dakota around Sisseton and Webster, for example, have had years of positive pheasant growth. While the numbers still may not be as high as traditional grounds, the birds are there.

(LEFT) Pheasants flush at the Harold Krage Ranch northeast of Aberdeen. Pheasants are the primary crop on Harold's ranch, which is managed for pheasants and has more birds than you could shake a gun at.

(RIGHT) Laurie Lauing serves home cooking at Dakota Hills Lodge in Oral, South Dakota.

Many of the public land opportunities here are of the wetland-type, and that means tremendous habitat.

Southeastern

The southeast region is home to that pheasant "triangle." It also houses Sioux Falls, the state's largest city, Mitchell, Chamberlain, Yankton, and other communities that can hold their own when it comes to pheasant hunting opportunities.

The largest concentrations of birds are found in this region. Annual brood counts in the Chamberlain area show a five-year mean of 13.2 birds per mile. The Mitchell area has a mean of almost seven birds per mile and the Winner area has a mean of six.

Great Lakes

The Missouri River and the Great Lakes Region of South Dakota are excellent choices as well. The U.S. Army Corps of Engineer lands along the Missouri River provide gunning opportunities, and with a map, these areas are easy to cover and for the most part are free from hunting pressure.

The Great Lakes Region, with five-year means ranging from 4.2 birds per mile in the Pierre area to 3.4 birds per mile in the Mobridge area, holds the potential to add grouse and prairie chickens to the game bag. The Harrold area west of Pierre is a choice destination. The Tumbleweed Lodge south of Harrold is a wingshooters' paradise.

(LEFT) Habitat consisting of crops, ditch banks, and shelter belts at Dakota Hills Lodge provides excellent shooting for ringnecks, Hungarians, and sharptails.

(RIGHT) Happy hunters, the Com South Group at Dakota Hills Lodge.

Some lesser-known areas in this region include the Philip area in west-central South Dakota. Recent years have seen bird populations increase. The area is mainly ranchland, but the potential to harvest grouse, prairie chickens, and pheasants is on the rise.

Black Hills/West River

While western South Dakota is a ways from the prime pheasant country, enough opportunities exist to make it worthwhile. Especially in those counties near the western shores of the Missouri River. Often very remote country, the countryside seems to extend beyond the horizon. And many times, just beyond that horizon, lies a pheasant hotbed waiting to be discovered. Dried-up creek beds, wafts of grasslands, and other heavy-habitat-laden areas can hold birds and not just pheasants. These areas offer a variety of game, where large coveys of grouse on one field's end to huge pheasant flushes on the other, are not uncommon.

Often seen only as a vacation destination, the Black Hills of South Dakota has pockets of huntable pheasants. The Oral area near the southern Black Hills of South Dakota is one of the top pheasant-producing areas.

With any area, the key is habitat and access to that area. It may take a little research to find that perfect spot, but it can be done.

Regardless of the ultimate destination, one trick is to take advantage of late-season birds—late November and December. Fewer hunters travel to South Dakota during this time, and it's much easier to gain access to private land as many residents have put away their shotguns for the year.

With open arms

South Dakota communities are very hospitable to hunters. "Welcome Hunters" signs adorn most merchants' doors during the season. Communities treat the pheasant opener and the season as a holiday, with high spirits at every turn. Many businesses hire additional help during the season to keep up with the hunters. The atmosphere is festive, with community breakfasts and welcoming gifts waiting for hunters. Dogs are more than welcome and many times they get treats as well.

Many community leaders, such as Pam Van Dover of the Corn Palace (Mitchell) Convention and Visitor's Bureau, are just as excited with the onset of pheasant season as the hunters are. "Mitchell streets are teaming with thousands of visitors during the vacation season, but during the hunting season, hunters come in a sea of orange in search of the wily ring-necked pheasant. It's simply wonderful to see all the hunters come in from all over the country to not only hunt pheasants but also to also take in what Mitchell and South Dakota have to offer. And we roll out the "orange carpet" to greet each and every one of them."

(OPPOSITE, BOTTOM LEFT) The Mitchell Chamber of Commerce welcomes hunters.

(OPPOSITE, BOTTOM RIGHT) A giant painting of a rooster on the side of a bus advertises Pair-A-Dice Ranch south of Miller, South Dakota.

(TOP LEFT) *The new Cabela's store in Mitchell, South Dakota.*

(TOP RIGHT) *David Richards, a globetrotting sportsman, wears a pheasant hunter's hat.*

(ABOVE) *The famous Corn Palace in Mitchell.*

Recommended guides, lodges, and information sources

KANSAS

DON'S GUIDE SERVICE LLC

Contact Don Zahourek
308 N. Hobart Street
Glen Elder, Kansas 67446
Phone (785) 545 3351 Cell (785) 545 5651
E-mail: kansashunting@nckcn.com
Website: www.kansashunting.net

Don has available 5,000 acres, which includes 640 preserve acres. The hunting is for wild, early release, and preserve pheasants. Lodging is provided in two separate houses and can accommodate up to 24 hunters. Packages include lodging, guide service, and hunting over German shorthair pointers (does not include meals). Wild birds include pheasants, bobwhite quail, and greater prairie chickens. **Don's Guide Service is featured on pages 102 and 104.**

ROCKBRANCH HUNTING LODGE

Anthony and Karensa Francka
Rt. 2 Box 64
Norton, KS 67654
Phone: (785) 877-3785
E-mail: rbranch@us36.net
Website: www.rockbranch.net

Rockbranch Lodge is a place to escape for a day or a weekend of some of the finest traditional pheasant hunting in Kansas. You'll hunt **FAST FLYING, WILD PHEASANTS** on 5,000 acres of private land flourishing with wild prairie grasses and rich crops. You'll wake up to hearty country style breakfasts each morning and return to a relaxing evening at the lodge after the hunt. If traveling, your lodging package will include **ONE FREE NIGHT'S ACCOMMODATION.** You can also book a packaged hunt for deer and predators.

MONTANA

EAGLE NEST LODGE

John and Rebecca Shirley
PO Box 509
Hardin, MT 59034
Phone: (866) 258-3474
E-Mail: flyfishmt@sbcglobal.net
Website: www.eaglenestlodge.com

Eagle Nest Lodge is the first lodge in the world to be dual endorsed by **Orvis for both Wing shooting and Fly Fishing.** Hunt Pheasant, Sharptail Grouse and Hungarian Partridge across the rolling hills of Montana. Fly Fish the famed Bighorn River which holds more fish per mile than any river in the lower 48 states. Add to this the serenity of a finely appointed log lodge and gourmet country dining and you'll have to agree Eagle Nest truly has it all. Guests are treated to a complimentary round of sporting clays and fisherman are pampered with the use of all ORVIS equipment included in their package price. Combine fly fishing and wing shooting for the ultimate outdoor experience!

NORTH DAKOTA

TTT RANCH

Fred & Joyce Evans
4949 Triple T rd.
Stanley, ND 58784
Phone: (701) 628-2418
E-mail: hunting@TTTranch.com
Website: www.TTTranch.com

"Perfection is our goal, Excellence is our standard." The TTT ranch, in the outback of America, is prime and pristine, truly a hunter's paradise. The ranch headquarters is nestled in the Little Knife River Valley, its waterway meanders through the broad valley with spacious coulees fanning out on either side providing abundant natural wildlife habitat. **It is simply the best in North Dakota.**

We customize the hunt to your parties' request. Come with a crew of 4 to 8 hunters and the ranch is yours for the duration of your stay! Starting in late August, the TTT ranch offers a variety of activities. Along with the Pheasant hunts, there is early season fishing on Lake Sakkakawa, and Golf at Red Mike's, one of America's great authentic links. Later in the season you can hunt pheasants, waterfowl, turkey, and archery hunt for whitetail deer. **"It's first class service with pie at every meal!"**

SOUTH DAKOTA

ABERDEEN VISITORS BUREAU

PO Box 78
Aberdeen, South Dakota 57402-0078
Phone: 1-800-645-3851 Fax: (605) 225-3573
E-Mail: info@aberdeencvb.com
Website: www.aberdeencvb.com

Aberdeen is in the heart of some of South Dakota's best pheasant and waterfowl hunting. When Dale C. Spartas hunted the Aberdeen area, he saw more pheasants than he'd ever imagined. To prolong the hunt he would kill one bird over each dog, return to the car to put another dog on the ground, and harvest a bird over that dog. The hunting was virtually "too good," if there is such a thing.

ANDERSEN FARMS HUNTING

PO Box 143
44923 201st St.
Badger, SD 57214
(605) 983-5807
E-mail: hunting@andersenfarms.com
Website: www.andersenfarms.com

Andersen Farms provides a premium, all inclusive South Dakota pheasant hunt designed to be a cut above other lodge hunts. The main package caters to small groups of up to 6 hunters and consists of a 3 day/ 4 night, fully guided, hunt on thousands of 4th generation acres that includes unique lodging, meals and services. You'll experience the hunt over professionally trained Pointing Labs from Andersen Farms Kennels. Airport pickup, trap shooting and bird cleaning included. There is also a private airport on the farm. Unguided hunts are also available on our Ricochet property, called **"The Best Hunting in South Dakota"** by former SD Lt. Governor Lowell Hansen!! Private. Exclusive. Andersen Farms. A Cut Above!

AmericInn LODGE AND SUITES

Chamberlain, SD
1981 East King Street
P.O. Box 654
Chamberlain, SD 57325
Contact: Jon A. Smith (800) 807-2376
E-Mail: aeromason1@sbcglobal.net
Website: www.americinnchamberlainsd.com

AmericInn Lodge and Suites in Chamberlain, South Dakota offers everything plus more for your hunting needs. In the heart of the best pheasant hunting South Dakota has to offer you will experience world-class pheasant hunting on 36,000 acres of private land. We offer guided hunts that include your room, guide and processing of birds starting at $225.00 and up per person, per day. You will have the option of staying in one of the suites or in an oversized room with two queen-sized beds. In the morning you will find a very appetizing complimentary deluxe breakfast bar. After hunting all day enjoy the complimentary happy hour each evening with beverages and appetizers, while relaxing in the pool, hot tub and sauna area. For events or meetings consisting of large groups the lodge does have a room fit to hold up to 25 people.

*"Wow! What a great November hunt! I wanted to once again thank you for the latest remarkable South Dakota Pheasant hunting experience. I am more impressed each time you guide our hunts. From the frequent shooting action to very comfortable lodging, you definitely have the talent to take care of both the big and the little details! Your hospitality and extra efforts make all the difference. **My father was especially pleased with how you tailored the hunt to the wide range of age and skills in our group.** I am finalizing the details for our trip next year!" —Jay Johnson, Lake Elmo MN (651) 351-0811*

*"Thank you very much for the pheasant hunt that we will soon not forget. We had a great time and were very impressed with your constant desire to take care of the hunters in your group. You are a true professional. **I sent an e-mail to the editor of Pheasants Forever regarding our excellent hunt!** —Darrel C. Smith, Executive Vice President, First Nebraska Financial Services Inc. (308) 534-1322*

BUFFALO BUTTE RANCH, LLC

Marshall and Colleen Springer
33376 Buffalo Butte Rd.
Gregory, SD 57533
Phone: (800) 203-6678
E-mail: springer@gwtc.net
Website: www.buffalobutte.com

Buffalo Butte combines WILD PHEASANT hunting with world class lodging in the heart of pheasant country known as the Golden Triangle. Hunt wild pheasants, turkey, prairie chicken, sharp-tail grouse, prairie dog, coyote or buffalo on over 6,000 acres of managed private land. Up to 20 hunters can sleep comfortably in the 4200 sq. ft. lodge. Amenities include: clay targets, kennels, bird processing, transportation on the hunt, fully stocked upper end bar, complimentary house wines and meals featuring western cuisine!

DAKOTA HILLS HUNTING LODGE

Contact Tom or Laurie Lauing
HC 56 Box 90
Oral, South Dakota 57766
Phone 1-800 622-3603 Cell (605) 890-9264
E-Mail: dakhills@gwtc.net
Website: www.dakotahills.com

Dakota Hills Hunting Lodge provides wild bird, early release, and preserve pheasant, chukar, and Hungarian partridge. With more than 5,000 acres of managed habitat, excellent wild bird populations, and a 1,200-acre preserve, Dakota Hills offers shooting from September 1 to March 31. The comfortable lodge has a game room, hot tub, and top-shelf bar. The package includes breakfast, lunch, and dinner, specializing in western cuisine. Other amenities are sporting clays, trap, a kennel to house your dogs, and well-trained German shorthairs, Labradors, and Springer spaniels. Dakota Hills Hunting Lodge is featured on pages 89, 119, and 120.

DAKOTA RIVER RANCH

Contact: Jeff Youngberg
PO Box 84
Columbia, SD 57433
Phone: (877) 228-0012 (605) 229-0012
E-mail: info@dakotariverranch.com
Website: www.dakotariverranch.com

At Dakota River Ranch you'll get a memorable, world-class experience tailored to meet your needs.

You'll stay in our 6200 sq. ft. lodge fit to accommodate up to 18 guests and comes equipped with sporting clays, horseshoes, game tables and satellite television. You'll hunt wild Pheasants on 10,000 acres of land that has been intensely managed for all types of wildlife. You'll hunt with an experienced guide over professionally trained dogs, or you're welcome to bring your own well-trained hunting companion. 5% of what you spend goes to a human suffering charity of your choice.

DAKOTA SKIES

Contact: Joe Krizan
PO Box 104
Humboldt, SD 57035
Phone: (605) 363-3883
E-Mail: info@dakota-skies.com
Website: www.dakota-skies.com

When you're ready for the hunting experience of a lifetime, look no further than Dakota Skies outfitters for the ultimate hunting experience! Located in the very heart of the South Dakota Pheasant belt, Dakota Skies offers the best hunting of wild pheasants available anywhere. Your hunting party will enjoy exclusive access to a professionally guided, wild pheasant hunt on over 2000 acres of private farmland. Your hunt includes everything from your hunting licenses and shells, to lodging and delicious prepared meals. Hunt Dakota Skies and let the adventure begin!

E CIRCLE E HUNTING FARMS

Contact: Steve Blythe or Robert S. Emmick
45345 311th Street
Meckling, SD 57044
Phone: (605) 624 2800 (605) 677-7925
E-mail: ecirclee@aol.com
Website: www.ecirclee.com

E Circle E Hunting Farms is a Certified Cabela's Wing-shooting Adventure. You'll experience one of the finest pheasant hunting operations southeast South Dakota has to offer. Hunt for a day or take advantage of the 3-day package which includes a mixed bag of pheasants and Hungarian partridge, lodging, meals, refreshments, licenses, bird cleaning, trap and skeet range, guides, shells, dogs and airport transportation. Unwind after the hunt in the hot tub or in front of the big screen TV.

ECHO VALLEY RANCH

Ron and Lynn Ogren
23249 376th Ave.
Wessington Springs, SD 57382
E-mail: ronogren@sbtc.net
Website: www.echovalleyranch.com

Nestled in the Wessington Spring hills, we have over 6500 acres in the heart of **Wild Pheasant** Country. We are **NOT** a preserve—you will find **WILD BIRDS** in our creek bottoms, shelterbelts, native grass stands and our challenging and creatively placed food plots. Being a family owned and operated business, we take great pleasure in providing your exclusive group with personal attention, private lodging, fantastic meals and professional guides with their own dedicated dogs. Want to hunt your own dog? You bet!! The lodge is comfortable and rustic with a game room, clay pigeon practice area and privacy. Contact us for specific packages and pricing!

MIKE KUCHERA'S SOUTH DAKOTA GUIDE SERVICE, INC.

Contact: Mike Kuchera
PO Box 10 Mitchell, SD 57301
135 East 2nd Ave, Mitchell, SD 57301
Phone: (605) 996-1120
Fax: (605) 996-1232
E-mail: mkuchera@sdpheasants.com
Website: www.sdpheasants.com

A TRADITION OF EXCELLENCE SINCE 1972! "It's a South Dakota Bird Hunting Safari!!" As seen on ESPN and OLN, we are well known for hunting the **WILD RINGNECK PHEASANTS** in south central South Dakota. Two and three day complete packages include: deluxe hotel/motel accommodations, all meals, including hot field buffet lunches, guides, professionally trained hunting dogs, ammunition, etc. You will hunt different farms each day in all types of cover. Other hunts available: Sharp-tail Grouse/Prairie Chicken and international hunting expeditions to New Zealand and Scotland.

MITCHELL SOUTH DAKOTA VISITORS BUREAU

601 N. Main St., Mitchell, South Dakota 57301
Phone: 1-866-273-2676 Fax (605) 996-8273
E-Mail: cvb@cornpalace.com
Website: www.cornpalace.com

Mitchell, South Dakota, is a pheasant-hunter-friendly town. There is good hunting within miles of Mitchell to the north, east, south, and west. **Leader Hardware & Sporting Goods** (605) 996-0316 or **Cabela's** (605) 995-1575 sell licenses and can meet every pheasant hunter's need or desire. The **Kelly Inn** (605) 995-0500 and the **Hampton Inn** (605) 995-1575 are hunter-friendly and welcome dogs. There are a number of good restaurants as well as "Hunter's Breakfasts" available during the first two weeks of the season. Late-season hunting, although somewhat neglected, can be fantastic.

OTTO'S PHEASANT HAVEN

Dave Otto
38390 188th
Tulare, SD 57476
Lodge Phone: (605) 596-4366
Home Phone: (605) 596-4277
Arlen Jessen: (605) 596-4267

At Otto's Pheasant Haven you'll be hunting for birds that are Cagey, Seasoned, and *STRICTLY WILD!* You'll find them hiding in and around the food plots scattered amongst the 1,000 acres of their natural habitat. The lodging provides a country atmosphere with a relaxing setting and is available for groups of up to eight hunters. Packages include: Lodging, guides, sack lunches and bird cleaning.

PAUL NELSON FARM

Contact Paul and Cheryl Nelson
PO Box 183
Gettysburg, South Dakota 57442
Phone: (605)765-2469 Fax (605)765-9648
E-Mail: hunting@paulnelsonfarm.com
Website: www.paulnelsonfarm.com

"A LEGENDARY WING SHOOTING ESTABLISHMENT"—Wall Street Journal.

Paul Nelson Farm combines world-class lodging and dining with the fast-and-furious pheasant gunning that South Dakota is famous for. Guests roam 12,000 acres of prime habitat, all within a five-minute drive of the lodge. Accommodations are for 34 people with single-and double-occupancy bedrooms, each with its own bath. It has wild, early release, and preserve pheasants and Huns. **Paul Nelson Farm** is an Orvis-endorsed Wingshooting Lodge.

PHEASANT CITY LODGE

Contact: Kevin Teveldal and sons Tryell, Tate or T Jay
36930 219th St.
Wessington, SD 57381
Phone: (605) 539-9244
E-Mail: hunt@pheasantcity.com
Website: www.pheasantcity.com

Pheasant City Lodge is a family owned operation located in the beautiful landscape of East-Central South Dakota. The endless span of wild prairie grass is full of upland birds and will provide an awesome **wild pheasant hunting experience! Everything you need is on location and part of your hunting package.** Bring your gun, your gear, and get ready for the hunt of a lifetime! You'll stay in our lodge large enough to sleep 28 people and comfortable enough to relax in after a day in the field.

REDLIN FARMS

Contact: Wally and Jeanne Redlin
PO Box 871
Summit, SD 57201
Wally: (605) 886-7177 (605) 880-7177
Frank: (605) 881-2479
Website: www.redlinfarms.com

At **Redlin Farms you customize your hunt to your satisfaction!** You and your partners will hunt 4000 acres of private grassland that was developed strictly for the **wild pheasant.** You'll also have the opportunity to add **sharptail grouse** and **Hungarian partridge** to your game bag. You'll be treated to first class lodging with all private rooms, or you may choose to stay in the bed and breakfast. There is great **walleye and perch fishing nearby along with excellent late season big game and waterfowl hunting.** You'll hunt with experienced guides over well-trained dogs!

SOUTH DAKOTA DEPARTMENT of TOURISM

1-800-SDAKOTA
E-Mail: sdinfo@state.sd.us
Website: www.travelsd.com

The South Dakota Department of Tourism can answer most of your questions and provide you with a list of lodges, guides, and outfitters, Hunter Walk In Areas, hunting seasons and regulations, and Convention and Visitor Bureaus (CVBs) listings.

THUNDERSTIK LODGE ROOSTER RIDGE LODGE

Contact: Gage Outdoor Expeditions
24931 Thunderstik Road
Chamberlain, SD 57325
Phone: (800) 888-1601
E-mail:hunting@gageoutdoor.com
Website: www.thunderstik.com

Thunderstik Lodge is proud to be **an Orvis Endorsed Wing Shooting Lodge.**

You'll experience some of the finest pheasant hunting in South Dakota amongst sweeping prairie vistas along the broad blue back of the majestic Missouri. You'll hunt thousands of acres of premier pheasant habitat including expansive shelter belts, native prairie grasses and assorted row crops. After the day's hunt enjoy five-star, all-inclusive accommodations at **Thunderstik Lodge** or private group accommodations at **Rooster Ridge.**

TUMBLEWEED LODGE

Contact Michael or Don Bollweg
20239 321st Avenue
Harrold, South Dakota 57536
Phone: 1-800-288-5774 Fax: (605) 875-3404
E-Mail: michael@tumbleweedlodge.com
Website: www.tumbleweedlodge.com

Tumbleweed Lodge offers elegant lodging, fine dining, a well-appointed complimentary bar, and fantastic hunting for **wild** birds and early release and preserve pheasants and Huns. Tumbleweed has 10,000 managed acres with a 1,700-acre hunting preserve open from September 1 to March 31. One may hunt the "Dakota Grand Slam" consisting of **Hungarian partridge, prairie chicken, sharptail grouse** and **pheasants.** Other amenities and activities include goose hunting, sporting clays, kennels, and vacuum-packed game processing. **Tumbleweed Lodge is featured on pages 29, 68, 69, 119, and in the introduction.**

VEURINK'S DAKOTA OUTDOORS

Contact Cal or Karen Veurink
38046 272nd Street
Harrison, South Dakota 57344
Phone (605) 946-5786 Cell (605) 481-1774
E-Mail: cal@hunt-dakota-outdoors.com
Website: www.hunt-dakota-outdoors.com

Veurink's Dakota Outdoors offers walleye fishing, turkey hunting, bow hunting for mule and whitetail deer, ducks over decoys, goose hunting on tribal lands, and **wild bird pheasant hunting.** Veurink's has more than 10,000 acres of land that is managed for wild bird production, resulting in excellent hunting. Veurink's is a family-run business with a family-like atmosphere. The comfortable lodge accommodates 16 guests has 4 bathrooms, TV, full kitchen, cleaning facilities, and kennels for your dogs. Their package includes lunch. Breakfasts and dinners are served at nearby diners and restaurants, or you can cook your own. **Veurink's Dakota Outdoors'is featured on pages 3, 4, 5 and 96.**

ABOUT THE PHOTOGRAPHER

Dale C. Spartas is an award-winning photographer specializing in hunting, fishing, sporting dogs, and the outdoors. More than 5,000 of his images have appeared in books, calendars, and magazines, including more than 135 cover photos for *Pheasants Forever Magazine, Gun Dog Magazine, Wing & Shot Magazine, Field & Stream, Outdoor Life, Fly Fisherman, American Angler,* and many others. He is a Contributing Photographer for *Sports Afield* and *Gray's Sporting Journal.* His books include *Just Labs* (Benjamin Franklin Photography Award winner), *Just Goldens, 101 Uses for a Lab, The Little Book of Fly Fishing,* and *To the Point, A Tribute to Pointing Dogs.* He lives in Bozeman, Montana.

Pheasants Forever—Making a difference

Join the growing number of people who are making a difference for pheasants and other wildlife. Since inception in 1982, Pheasants Forever has had a monumental impact on upland conservation. But much remains to be done! Do your part by becoming a member today and you will ensure the future of ringneck pheasant and other wildlife.

Who we are
- Over 100,000 grassroots members and volunteers who have developed more than 2.7 million acres of pheasant and other wildlife habitat since inception
- 600 chapters completing over 25,000 projects annually
- More than 4,000 educators promoting conservation through the Leopold Education Project
- A vast network of individual and corporate contributors.

What we do
- Protect, restore, and enhance wildlife habitat by establishing and maintaining local and regional projects
- Develop, distribute and foster conservation education
- Introduce and advance prudent conservation policy
- Acquire and preserve critical habitat through public land acquisition open to public hunting

Pheasants Forever
1783 Buerkle Circle
St. Paul, Minnesota 55110
Call toll free 1-877-773-2070
www.pheasantsforever.org

THE WRITERS IN *ROOSTER!*

The Thing About Pheasants
Michael McIntosh, Contributing Editor and Shooting Editor, *Shooting Sportsman Magazine*

The Pheasant Life
Jim Wooley, Pheasants Forever Senior Wildlife Biologist and 2002 Jeffery S. Finden Conservation Achievement Award winner

Tradition: Hunting With Friends and Family
Jim Wooley

Pheasant Dogs
Dave Carty, Western Region Editor, *Hartland USA Magazine*; Retriever Columnist, *Ducks Unlimited Magazine*

Guns and Shooting
Ron Spomer, Field Editor, *American Hunter Magazine*; Senior Editor, *Sporting Classics Magazine*

Three Seasons in One
Ron Spomer

Pheasants Now and Forever
Mark Herwig, Editor of *Pheasants Forever Magazine*

Hunting Tips
Bill Benson, Larry Brown, Dave Carty, Joe Duggan, Jeff Finden, Paul Hanson, Mark Herwig, Craig Janssen, Dr. Bill Long, Jerry Robinson, Dale C. Spartas, Ron Spomer, Michael Pearce, Kenny Snyder, Janet VanDerBeek, Cal Veurink, Howard Vincent, Berdette Zastrow, and others

Hunting in the Top States
Nebraska by David Draper, Field Editor for *Cabela's Outfitter Journal*
North Dakota by Dan Nelson, Editor, *Delta Waterfowl Magazine*
South Dakota by Lee Harstad, South Dakota Department of Tourism
Kansas by Michael Pearce, Outdoor Writer and Photographer for The Wichita Eagle

Iowa by Larry Brown, Training Columnist for *Pointing Dog Journal*
Minnesota by Michael Furtman, author of *On the Wings of a North Wind* and 2003 Ducks Unlimited Communicator of the Year.

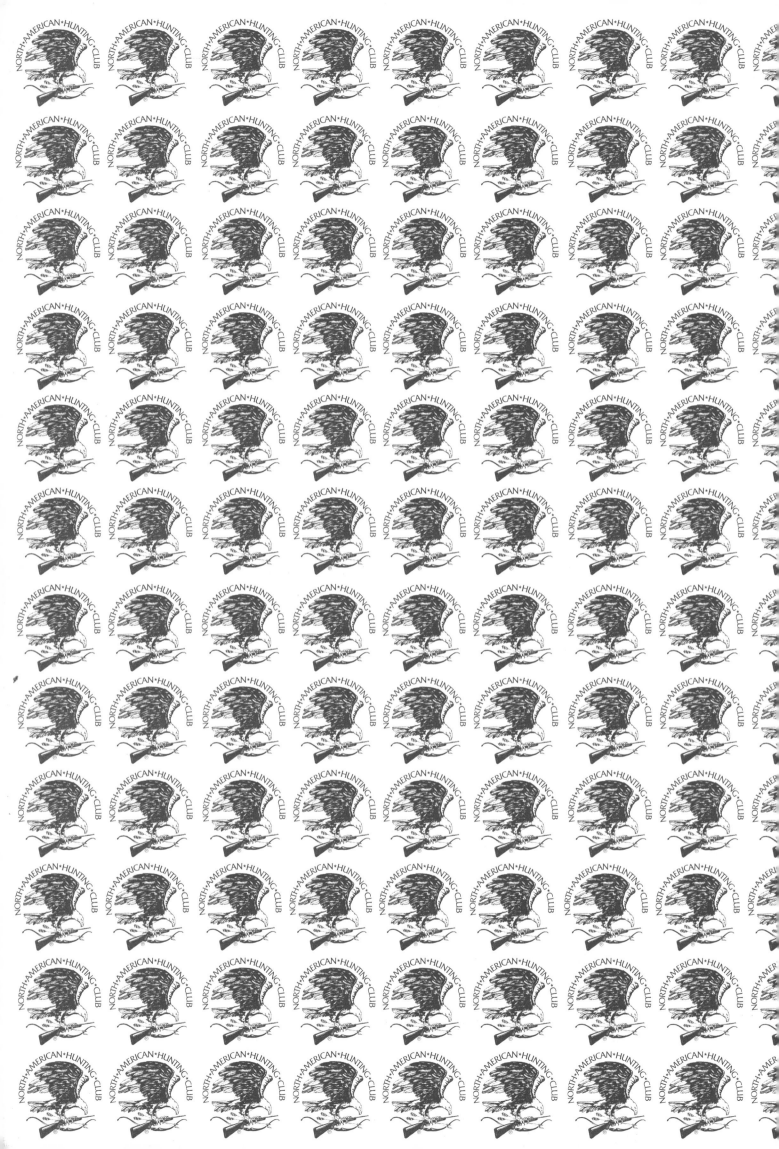